N E A N

S E A

BRITAIN IN THE WESTERN MEDITERRANEAN

HUTCHINSON'S UNIVERSITY LIBRARY

BRITISH EMPIRE HISTORY

EDITOR:

SIR REGINALD COUPLAND

K.C.M.G., C.I.E., M.A., D.LITT.

Late Beit Professor of the History of the British Empire in the University of Oxford

BRITAIN IN THE WESTERN MEDITERRANEAN

by

W. F. MONK M.A.

SENIOR HISTORY LECTURER, VICTORIA
UNIVERSITY COLLEGE, NEW ZEALAND

HUTCHINSON'S UNIVERSITY LIBRARY
Hutchinson House, London, W.1.
New York   Toronto   Melbourne   Sydney   Cape Town

First Published - 1953

To

SIR JAMES HIGHT

Printed in Great Britain by
William Brendon and Son, Ltd.
The Mayflower Press (late of Plymouth)
at Bushey Mill Lane
Watford, Herts.

CONTENTS

PREFACE

I cannot take leave of this study without expressing at once my thanks and my apologies. The thanks are due to the many who have helped me with their time and with their criticism. In particular, I should like to mention the editor of this series, Sir Reginald Coupland, for his patient encouragement; Prof. Vincent Harlow, who first directed my researches into the field of British Mediterranean policy; my wife and Mr. Anthony Bridbury, who gave their great help in the critical drafting stages; Miss Elizabeth Poyser and Mr. C. Willis Dixon, who advised on particular aspects; Miss B. McLean, of Marsden School, Wellington, who drew the contour map; Prof. F. L. W. Wood, who did gallant rescue work with the proofs; and the Librarians of the London Library, the Royal Empire Society, and Westminster School (where this book was written).

The apologies are due to students of colonial history because, in a field which has been neglected by historians, I can offer, to fill the void, no more than an introductory essay. For my main thesis on the other hand, I offer no apology. I have merely made explicit what has long been implicit in the writings of historians of foreign and naval policy.

Victoria University College,
    Wellington, New Zealand.

INTRODUCTION

Two things may be noticed about the Mediterranean. One is
the fact that it pushes so deeply into the land mass as to divide
Africa from Europe and Asia, thereby converting Europe itself
into a peninsula which, through its subsidiary peninsulas and
seas, islands and rivers, is peculiarly accessible to sea power.
The other is the fact that of all the nations of the modern world
which might have exercised naval power in that great warm sea
the one to do so with most success and over the longest period
has been Britain. Why Britain has been able or allowed to do
this may be variously explained. What is certain is that her
resolve to do so ranks high among the factors that enabled her
to become a great imperial nation.

The story of Britain in the Western Mediterranean is
accordingly of interest in several ways. In so largely determining
her achievement elsewhere, her policy there also largely reflected
her growth as nation and empire. To be able to exert power at all,
she had to expand her trade. That within the Mediterranean
was one of the first and most important of her distant trades;
and when, at length, it was surpassed in value by greater trades
beyond it, control of the Mediterranean became even more
important, for along it lay the highway *via* Suez to the East.

Strategically, likewise, Britain soon found that she could
defeat rivals like Spain and France by taking advantage of their
peninsular position and throttling them with sea power. These
nations frequently acted as one. By acquiring continental allies
to engage their Eastern front, and bases in Lisbon, Gibraltar
and Minorca to divide their naval effort, Britain was able to
use her own resources to maximum advantage while reducing
theirs to a minimum. With the rise of Germany this power plan
scarcely altered. In the face of national instinct and tradition
Britain bent to circumstances, allied with her recent enemy in

the West, and reduced her latest enemy by the same grim process of encirclement and strangulation. Even when, as during the three eighteenth-century wars, she acted ineffectually in the Mediterranean, she still applied these principles as best she could; though in each case her resources were diverted across the Atlantic to gains and commitments in the Americas.

To maintain her position in the Mediterranean, Britain was obliged to have allies and naval bases there. While Italy remained a geographical expression, allies were readily found in the houses of Savoy and Austria, both of whom needed the support of sea power to sustain them against Spain and France. When Italy became united, she remained vulnerable to sea power, and Britain looked instinctively to her as a natural ally against France and Germany.

The ideal naval base not only has a secure harbour and port but is at once well placed strategically, virtually impregnable, and not without economic resources. Britain was fortunate in finding in Lisbon (an essential approach), Tangier, Gibraltar, Minorca and Malta bases which very nearly fulfilled these conditions. It will be noticed that the spearhead of British power was pressed eastward in step with the shift of European hegemony until in the nineteenth century Malta, or even Alexandria, assumed the leading role. In keeping with this policy, moreover, Britain did not flinch from sharing her Mediterranean predominance with her recent enemy, France, or, latterly, with the United States.

Apart from Tangier and Gibraltar, the possession of bases in the Mediterranean involved Britain in problems new to her in colonial government. The Mediterranean islanders were not primitive peoples who could be subjected or tutored, but proud and individualistic heirs of a civilization more ancient than Britain's own. To govern them satisfactorily at all would have been difficult enough. The problem was complicated by the need to satisfy commercial interests at home and on the spot, while at the same time maintaining military security. British colonial policy probably has not owed much to a Mediterranean experience which chiefly confirmed lessons learnt elsewhere. But British policy in the Mediterranean did closely reflect changing trends. Beginning with eighteenth-century ideas of considerable local self-government within the mercantile framework, it fell back in the Napoleonic era on the socially unsuitable but militarily desirable despotic Crown Colony rule. Then slowly it evolved towards a new democratic freedom only limited by the most obvious needs of local welfare and imperial security.

CHAPTER I

FOUNDATIONS OF A POLICY:
BEGINNINGS TO 1688,
TANGIER

WHEN Britain first made her influence felt in the Mediterranean early in the seventeenth century, that sea was still dominated by the conflict of Cross and Crescent. Apart from one or two Spanish outposts in North Africa, its entire coastline from Morocco to Dalmatia was under Turkish sway; and Turkey's European frontier extended to Buda-Pesth and the head of the Adriatic. Christendom's bulwark against this danger was the Hapsburg monarchy, divided between the Empire, which guarded the Danube, and the kingdoms of Spain and the two Sicilies which, with the Balearic Islands and Sardinia, opposed a ravaged maritime frontier to the corsair galleys from northern Africa. Breasting the main current of Turkish advance, in the defile between Sicily and Tunis, lay the small island of Malta. This was now the home of the crusading order of the Knights of St. John who had been given it by the Hapsburg Emperor, Charles V, in 1530. The Great Siege which they withstood in 1565 had stemmed one reach of the Turkish tide; and they were now converting Valletta into an impregnable fortress and port. Their efficient and uncompromising opposition to the Turk was, indeed, one of the few certain factors in Europe's defensive system.

The other Christian powers were less stalwart champions. The Ionian Islands and Crete belonged to the Republic of Venice, whose seven or more centuries of commercial contact with Islam had been the secret of her greatness. France, similarly, found alliance with the infidel a useful precaution against whatever power threatened her eastern frontier as well as profitable to her Marseilles merchants. Furthermore, Christian Europe was not itself united. To Protestant Britain and Holland, now seeking their fortunes abroad, the menace of Islam seemed of less account; their interest being to profit by any weakness in the Counter-Reformation position, which in their eyes dominated the world at large in much the same way as the Turk did the smaller world of the Mediterranean. They were thus enabled to reap a harvest of trade and strategic power in the centre and east of that sea.

Between 1603, when the first Stuart ascended the English throne, and the Stuart Restoration in 1660, the contest between the forces of Counter Reformation and Reformation, of Hapsburg world empire and the opposition to it, was fought to a conclusion in the Thirty Years War and the Franco-Spanish struggle which succeeded it (1618-59). While the first Stuarts reigned official Britain was too enfeebled by internal conflict to play any considerable part abroad. Nor had she yet learnt what naval power might do. Nevertheless, it was in these years that British and Dutch merchants established themselves in the Mediterranean trade.

Hitherto, British merchants had failed to make much headway in face of the Italian monopoly. In the 1580s, however, the newly founded Levant Company dropped agents in Algiers, Zante and Leghorn and began importing precious ostrich feathers, currants, oils, wines and silks. Leghorn being made a free port in 1593, it speedily grew into a great *entrepôt* of trade dominated by Dutch and English merchants; and though the Levant Company imported a proportion of its Turkey goods *via* Leghorn, it failed to maintain its monopoly there against the insistent "interloping" of other English merchants. Accordingly, before the middle of the century that port had become the chief distributing centre of Turkey goods and English cloth and the Company's keenest competitor. At the same time the new classes rising to power in England were beginning to see where their interest lay, and to experiment in Mediterranean affairs.

Naval interest in the Mediterranean arose as an unforeseen consequence of the peace concluded with Spain in 1604. Men who had been hoping for fortunes on the Spanish Main were obliged to seek a living elsewhere, and a number found it in the Turkish strongholds of Tunis and Algiers. Ruffians like the mutineer, Ward, sold their services to the beys and organized the pirate fleets on ocean-going lines. They terrorized the Western Mediterranean and effected a technical revolution by proving the supremacy of sail over oar in that sea. When Spain's exiled Moriscos set up their own corsair state at Salee on the Atlantic coast of Morocco in 1609, they were soon joined by English adventurers who founded another pirate state at Mehediya a bit to the north. Before many years had passed, the Barbary corsairs were ranging as far afield as Ireland and Newfoundland and constituting a threat which even the Atlantic nations could not ignore.

Britain replied with an expedition against Algiers in 1620-1 led by Sir Robert Mansell. The need to deal with the corsairs gave excuse at once to demonstrate British power and try out a sailing fleet in those seas. Significantly, though Mansell was allowed to use Gibraltar and Malaga as bases, he made little attempt to co-operate with the Spanish; while they, for their part, watched his activities with anxiety. As luck had it, when, after long delays, he turned to attack the corsairs, the wind dropped and rain came on just as the enemy ships were set alight. The first venture of the British navy into those historic seas was accordingly a failure.

However, when war broke out with Spain in 1625, the idea was followed up in an attempt to take Cadiz and use it as a base "to support and countenance our successive fleets". Such an object showed the dawning perception of a Mediterranean strategy. It drew forth, moreover, the proposal of Sir Henry Bruce that Gibraltar should be seized instead. Lightly defended, its New Mole but recently constructed to take broadside ships, Gibraltar might have been taken. If it could have been held, it would have covered the Levant trade and been a check on France as well. But the idea was not taken up by men still preoccupied with the rewards of pillage. The attempt on Cadiz itself foundering, it was left to others to draw their conclusions from the new developments.

The lead was taken by the French who, in 1626, began their challenge to Spain's Mediterranean supremacy with the construction of a naval base at Toulon and a bid to acquire Sicily and Naples as a strategic dependent kingdom. Thus the

Hapsburg lifeline, linking Spain with Italy and Germany, was threatened with the improved naval weapon.

Next, the Commonwealth, succeeding the Stuarts in Britain in 1648, took advantage of its formidable navy to win recognition abroad. Some of the fleet having gone over to Prince Rupert, the balance, led by Blake and Penn, chased him into the Mediterranean in 1650-1 as far as Toulon, and then right out again. It was the first time a British fleet wintered and refitted in the Mediterranean—using Spanish and Sicilian bases—and it was also the first time ships were specially assigned to convoy the Levant trade. In thus distinguishing between merchantmen and warships, the Commonwealth was effecting still another revolution in technique. Standing armies were never to be tolerated in Britain, but a navy always in being and with specialized functions was to become the chief instrument of national power.

When war broke out with Holland in 1652 a small Mediterranean squadron was based on Leghorn where Dutch and English merchants were competing fiercely. The port, being neutral, offered both sides equal access for careening and supply. The Dutch, however, were double the English strength and, supported from French ports, blockaded them in Leghorn. At last, in March 1652, the English were forced out for a breach of neutrality and shattered by the Dutch, who thereby gained control of Mediterranean waters. This was a blow to Britain's Levant trade, but as it made no difference to the outcome of the war it suggested the lesson that in a war with Holland control of the Mediterranean was of little account. Such a war had to be won in the Channel, and the Dutch were merely dissipating their strength by attacking trade.

Cromwell, becoming Protector in 1653, had larger policies in mind and brought this Dutch war to an end. The prayers of the Leghorn navy agent, Longland, were answered when, late in the summer of 1654, Blake was sent out again with twenty ships to show the flag and influence policy. Held up in the Straits, he nevertheless unwittingly scared back the French Brest fleet and thwarted without a blow a second attempt on the Two Sicilies. Welcomed in Leghorn, he went on to smash the Tunisian fleet under the Bey's own batteries and to receive from Algiers, warned by the example, a prompt release of captives and the renewal of an earlier treaty.

So far Blake had been cruising as if against France and receiving friendly treatment in Spanish ports. When he passed out of the Straits, however, in May 1655, word came of Penn's attack on the Spanish West Indies. So for the next four months he lay off Cadiz; and then, the utmost profit having been drawn from his show of power within the Straits, he took his worn ships home.

Cromwell thus sided, unwisely, with France, and the centre of war activity shifted to the Channel, where he secured Dunkirk. His gaze, however, did not leave the south. In 1656-7 Blake cruised again and, standing off Cadiz, gave careful thought to seizing Gibraltar or some other strong point within the Straits. In the end he only formed a victualling base at Tetuan on the Rif coast. With Lisbon available for careening no more was perhaps needed in a war against Spain alone. But his mere presence in the Straits again exerted its influence up the Mediterranean. His successor, Stoakes, was able to use Marseilles and thence cut the communication between Spain and Italy and exact favourable treaties from Tunis and Tripoli. By the time Cromwell died, in 1658, the mercantile classes in England were growing used to the idea of Mediterranean power.

Tangier

The Restoration of Charles II coincided with an eastward shift in the balance of European power. The Peace of the Pyrenees, in 1659, recorded the triumph of France over Spain and virtually disposed of the Hapsburg danger. In doing so, however, it made possible a Bourbon bid for European and world supremacy, which was not to be defeated for another century and a half. Between 1660 and 1815 Britain and France were at war with each other seven different times and for more than sixty years. As the value of Mediterranean power was increasingly realized by both sides, that sea became a normal scene of naval and economic conflict. For both powers alike supremacy there meant the ability to take the offensive against the other. Britain could encircle France by blockade and

B

diplomacy. France could concentrate her fleets to strike in the Channel or in the West or East Indies. Confronted with so capable, populous and well-administered a nation as the French, it was well for Britain that she enjoyed her island advantages, and that her rival was nearly always engaged on land as well as by sea.

Circumstances conspired to give Britain a temporary lead. Now Spain's hands were freed, the Portuguese, still struggling for their independence and looking round for help, found a British alliance attractive. Accordingly, in 1661, Charles was given the Princess Catherine in marriage with a dowry which included the fortress of Tangier. The Portuguese held Tangier precariously, but Britain might have the resources to hold and develop it. By giving up Dunkirk in favour of Tangier Charles correctly anticipated the course of Britain's future.

Tangier stands on the African shore of the Straits of Gibraltar. With the fortress of Tarifa on the Spanish coast opposite it forms a strategic quadrangle whose Mediterranean end is completed by Gibraltar and Ceuta. Since the Reconquest these had all been held against the Moors by the Portuguese and Spanish. The walls of Tangier spanned the valley between the crests of two low hills, and the city formed an amphitheatre which looked down steeply on a somewhat open bay. Higher hills lay behind and the place would hardly be safe unless these also were taken and fortified. Charles did not realize what this would cost.

Indeed, Charles had higher hopes of Tangier than of any other of his imperial possessions except, perhaps, Jamaica. About him were men of spirit and ideas who believed that by building a mole to protect the harbour from the Atlantic breakers Tangier could be made to shelter a fleet. England might then control the Straits, put down the corsairs and safeguard her Levant trade. She might even create an *entrepôt* like Leghorn and tap the rich interior. Or conquer from the Moors a British Empire of North Africa! As these commercial hopes were never realized and even a fortress was expected to pay, Tangier's real strategic advantages were sacrificed when it was given up.

Certainly Tangier had distinct disadvantages as a port and naval base. The great Mole, five hundred yards in length, had not been completed by the time of the evacuation in 1684. The Mediterranean squadron had to depend on Spanish ports for careening and refitting, though small vessels were being cleaned in Tangier in the early 'seventies. Nevertheless, the fact remained that there generally was a Mediterranean squadron and that it had a base of its own for victualling and supply which gave it the independence it needed. Moreover, once the mole had been pushed out a certain distance, the harbour afforded invaluable protection against the corsair in peace time, and became a rendezvous for Mediterranean and West Indian convoys in time of war.

Tangier was Britain's first colony of trade and arms. Considering her inexperience and her distance from the scene, she did not manage it badly. To hold it at all was an achievement. It had no resources of its own. The immediate environs were mainly sandhills and richer pasture had to be taken and held. The supply of fresh food depended on the goodwill of Moor and Spaniard. Basic supplies had to be brought out from England by a rough sea passage of anything from a fortnight to six weeks. Without command of the sea between the English Channel and the Straits Tangier could not have been held for more than a few months. In the circumstances it is less surprising that Charles gave it up when he did than that he clung to it for so long in face of pressing financial need.

The maker of British Tangier was Andrew Rutherford, Earl of Teviot, who arrived fresh from Dunkirk in 1663. Cast in an Elizabethan mould, he shared every hardship with his men and during his short governorship united the motley civilians and soldiers into a spirited community. The Moors declared that he never slept except leaning against his gun. He won the personal respect of the great Ghailan (Gayland), the predatory local chieftain, and earned the garrison a formidable reputation.

Teviot was skilled in the science of fortification; and under his direction the mole was begun, giving protection from the sea, the walls of the town were strengthened, and an outer line of defences begun among the surrounding hills. He raised and trained the Tangier Horse and developed among his men an ability in scouting equal to that of the Moors themselves. Although he was killed from ambush with a fifth of the garrison in May 1664, his successors continued his methods and "fighting with one hand and fortifying with the other", completed a fine system of strategic outposts which deterred the enemy for fourteen more years.

Under Teviot Tangier was ruled by prerogative, the governor issuing ordinances more or less in conformity with the laws of England. At home Teviot had to deal with a body known as the Committee for the Affairs of Tangier, virtually a committee of the Privy Council. Through its Treasurer, Samuel Pepys, this body arranged the victualling, supply and finance, but left questions of policy to the Privy Council proper. In practice, the affairs of Tangier seem to have been managed down to 1674, by the crypto-Catholic Lord Arlington. Through this man Charles used the requirements of "his city of Tangier" as an excuse for building up a small but efficient standing army and finding employment for Roman Catholic friends. In these circumstances the garrison was doomed to uncertain supply and a pernicious shortage of cash. The soldiers were sometimes two years behind in pay and essential works had often to be neglected through lack of materials.

It was primarily to meet this financial difficulty that a civil government was set up. On 4 June 1668 Tangier was incorporated by charter as a free city and given a mayor, six aldermen and twelve councillors with power to make laws for government and trade along the lines of English law. Revenue was drawn from rents, fines and excise duties and applied to the payment of civil salaries and public works. Justice was administered by civil and criminal courts which dealt with all except mercantile and military causes. The judges were the elected mayor and aldermen assisted by a legal adviser and, in criminal cases, by a jury. To encourage trade a special Court Merchant was set up. Elected from the merchants by the Corporation, it met daily and gave the requisite speedy decisions. Unfortunately it came into conflict with non-mercantile interests.

Such an establishment afforded some saving to the Crown, but was over-elaborate for so small a community. In a far-away garrison town there is always tension. In Tangier this was increased by the menace of enemies everywhere about and the presence of foreigners and spies within the walls. Commercial interests divided into factions and contended with the military and with one another. The first mayor had to fly to Spain for safety. Lord Middleton, who was governor from 1668-74, eased the situation a little by securing the election of an officer as mayor. The Corporation exercised its functions jealously and failed to provide many amenities. Its exclusion of foreigners from its offices combined with the stringent health regulations required for the Spanish trade, to impede the desired flow of commerce. However, in the 'seventies Tangier must still have seemed a promising centre of trade and power.

The resident civil population probably never exceeded six or seven hundred. Most of the Portuguese left the moment the English arrived rather than have truck with heretics. As they took with them everything they possessed down to the very "floors, windows and doores", the newcomers found themselves pioneers in a strange new land instead of sharing the life of an established commercial community. Difficulty was found in attracting "men of credit" but as a free port (1662) Tangier soon drew fortune hunters from different parts of the Mediterranean, as well as traders and seamen.

But Tangier's trade never fulfilled its promise. Cadiz merchants used the town as a base for some of their contraband activities. It became a terminus for the caravan trade by sea between Smyrna and Morocco and a market for English colonial timber and plantation produce. Some local fruit and wine was exported to England. But trade with the interior remained in the hands of Barbary Jews and was interrupted by the incessant hostilities with the Moors. Foreign merchants were discouraged by the scarcity of money and the jealous policy of the Corporation.

As a garrison town Tangier had to meet the needs of some two thousand uneducated soldiers and seamen, compelled to endure a hot climate and unhealthy conditions in a society bereft of decent women. Not unnaturally the number of wine houses, officially limited to twenty-four, rose to nearer a hundred, and the place got a bad reputation for drunkenness, disease and crime. The streets were narrow, crooked and insanitary, and the northerners' ways ill-adjusted to life in such a climate. Yet the town seems to have grown into an attractive spot. Built in the Spanish style, the houses were mainly two-storeyed, with almost flat, red-tiled roofs, stone or mud walls and glassless windows. Many of them had delightful private gardens, with vines and orange trees and sweet-scented flowers. Tangier even became the occasional resort of well-to-do visitors, noted for its hunting, fishing, balls and plays.

In the 'seventies, Tangier was mistakenly felt to be secure. The garrison had already been reduced in 1668 and now the defences were allowed to fall into disrepair. It was a serious error for, in 1672, there succeeded as Sultan the great Muley Ismael, who reigned until 1727 and was known as the Blood-thirsty. By 1676 Muley's lieutenants were closing in on the coastal outposts still held by Spain. Many had gained experience in the Eastern Mediterranean and, trained in the latest siege-craft, were far more formidable adversaries than those with whom Teviot had dealt.

The governor from 1674 to 1680 was Lord Inchiquin, who did his best to help trade but had little military capacity. Fortunately he was often absent and authority devolved on the self-made Palmes Fairborne, an officer of natural talent who had learnt his craft, like the Moors, in Crete and Tangier itself. Between 1678-9 the Moors cut off access to pasture and fuel. Between March and May 1680 they stormed the outer line of forts and got Inchiquin to agree to a truce which would have left the town an open battleground. Fairborne disregarded its terms, repaired the forts in his possession and secured the loan of two hundred Catalan Horse. When he had been reinforced and the truce expired in September 1680 he beat the Moors at their own technique of surprise and stratagem. Supported from the sea by Admiral Herbert, he recovered the key position known as Fort Pole, and before he died of wounds in October he watched his troops rout the Moors in a general sally from the town.

Muley Ismael now offered to negotiate and Charles sent out a special envoy to arrange the terms of peace. With him went Colonel Percy Kirke, who had brought out the newly raised Second Tangier Regiment. Something in Kirke's demeanour won Muley's heart, and he agreed to tolerable terms for four years, though only on condition that no new fortifications were erected. While the Sultan turned upon the Spanish, his

ambassador was received in England with every mark of wonder
and esteem and even elected an honorary member of the Royal
Society. The Whitehall Treaty was signed in March 1682. But
on his return to Morocco, the ambassador was disgraced and
the treaty repudiated.

Early the next year Charles decided he could no longer
afford the upkeep of Tangier. Freed from his dependence on
Parliament, he was not uninfluenced by the wish to have troops
nearer at hand. Nevertheless he resisted the temptation to ease
his purse by selling the fortress to Louis XIV, and proceeded
with caution so as not to let it fall into unsuitable hands.

Lord Dartmouth was given the task of evacuating the
inhabitants and garrison and effecting the demolitions. His fleet,
with Pepys on board, arrived off Tangier in September. The
work of blowing up the Mole on which so much skill and money
had been expended was undertaken by the engineer who had
built most of it, Henry Shere. It was like a man butchering his
own child, they said. It took three months to complete. After
that came the dangerous job of dismantling the land fortifications, levelling the town, and withdrawing the troops in face of
an enemy who became ever more menacing. While this was
going on the fleet paid cautionary visits to all the corsair strongholds and secured a general redemption of British slaves. When
it finally weighed anchor on 5 March 1684 and the Moors took
exultant possession of the debris, Britain ceased to be a
Mediterranean power.

One result of the possession of Tangier had been security
for British commerce at a time when Barbary depredations were
near their peak. The regular appearance of naval squadrons
inside the Straits induced the beys to keep on fair treaty terms
with Britain. They granted minimum rights to British subjects
living in their territories and agreed to respect the British
Mediterranean Pass authorized by the treaties of 1662. The
frequent accession of new rulers required in each case a further
exchange of presents, on the Barbary side exotic elephants or
Arab steeds, on the British more matter-of-fact powder and
guns. The multiplicity of counterfeit passes and other irregu-
larities made friction inevitable. But so long as Britain held a

base within the Straits from which her warships could operate, she was probably better treated than any other state; the price, however, was the negotiation, even in that short time, of as many as five separate treaties with Algiers alone.

The same period was also notable for the growth of trade with Spain and Italy. The Commercial Treaty with Spain of 1667 went far to restore a traditional flourishing connection. A special clause of the Navigation Act of 1660 permitted the importation of "Turkey goods" from Leghorn and certain other "privileged ports" in Italy. Leghorn continued to prosper, distributing great quantities of English cloth and salt fish and providing English shipping with rich return cargoes. English woollens also sold well in the now friendly Sicily and Sicilian wines and silks grew popular in England. Britain's actual or virtual neutrality in the several Mediterranean wars, her good relations with the corsairs and the influence of the Navigation Acts united to give her a predominant share in the Mediterranean carrying trade.

Although twice at war herself, once against Holland and France (1664-7) and then, in alliance with France, against Holland alone (1672-4) Britain was not misled into making the Mediterranean a major theatre. In each war both sides had big interests there, but neither could afford to disperse its strength. The lesson of the First Dutch War was driven home in 1666 when Louis XIV came to the assistance of the Dutch. Except for a relief squadron and her privateers acting from Tangier, Britain had no force to put in the way of the Toulon fleet, and the dispatch of Rupert to meet the danger left Monk to defeat in the tremendous Four Days' Battle in the Channel.

As Louis's power mounted, the good sense of the nation saw that its interest now lay with the Dutch and the Hapsburgs. Louis had made an unsuccessful bid in 1664 to establish a counterpart of Tangier at Jijelli; and it was in these years that Frenchmen first dreamed of empire in Egypt and a canal at Suez. In 1675 the revolt of Messina revived in Louis's mind the plan of Mazarin to control the Two Sicilies, and his navy, raised to a peak of excellence by Colbert and ably led by Duquesne, overcame the Dutch in Italian waters. In face of this expansion even Charles's pensioner government grew anxious.

The Duke of York's Protestant daughter, Mary, was married in 1677 to William of Orange; and a strong squadron entered the Straits. Though it based itself on Malta, ostensibly to act against the Tripolitan corsairs, its proximity persuaded Louis to withdraw his forces from Messina in 1678 before the peace was signed.

The same causes that led to the surrender of Tangier led also to the decay of the Navy and of Britain's influence abroad. Great events took place in Europe between 1683 and 1688, but Britain had no part in them. The Turks were finally repulsed from Vienna; Louis XIV made further progress on the Rhine and Moselle, and provoked yet another European alliance against him; French Protestantism was expunged. The invitation which Whigs and Tories united to extend to William of Orange in 1688 to accept the English Crown was accordingly not only due to detestation of James's despotism and Catholicism at home; it was also inspired by anxiety at Britain's helplessness abroad.

CHAPTER II

PURSUIT OF A BASE: GIBRALTAR AND MINORCA, 1689-1713

THE failure of the restored Stuarts had not been due to unawareness of what Britain's mercantile interests were. In that respect they had been worthy successors of the Commonwealth and Protectorate. Their error lay in valuing their personal independence above that of the nation. The Glorious Revolution became the Legend of later days just because it symbolized the surrender of the Crown to the service of the nation. Dutch William was far from being a nonentity. But he had learnt discretion in long experience of the burghers of Holland and, above all, he was a crusader in the cause of the Netherlands and Protestantism against Bourbon and Catholic France. His deepest interests therefore coincided with those of his English hosts.

One result of the Glorious Revolution was to involve Britain in William's war with France. This began, however, as a war for British survival and for the Protestant Succession. For French troops landed in Ireland in support of James II, a failure of sea power which seemed confirmed in 1690 when the combined navies of Britain and Holland gave way before the Brest and Toulon fleets off Beachy Head. England lying open to invasion, Louis assembled an army near Cherbourg. Though the immediate danger was removed in 1692 by Russell's victory of La Hogue, Louis's armies remained successful everywhere on land, in Flanders, on the Rhine, in Savoy and in Catalonia. The inadequacy of allied naval policy was driven home the next year by the loss of the "Smyrna convoy" bound for the Levant. This rich prize fell to the Brest fleet which Louis was transferring to the Mediterranean where he meant to turn his naval supremacy to decisive account. It was to counteract these French plans that Britain evolved that system of naval strategy which she has never since abandoned.

Most of the credit must go to William himself. In defence

of the Netherlands he had already had experience of encircling France with leagues of land powers; but experience showed that this was not enough. Holland's resources were being used up in the land warfare and she was no longer France's equal by sea. It was for this reason that William had given himself to Britain. The Grand Alliance included Austria, Spain, Savoy, and all the chief German states. With British and Dutch naval power united against her as well, France might not only be contained, as formerly, in Flanders and on the Rhine. The pressure of sea power might revive the drooping Spaniard and Savoyard, transform the situation in the Mediterranean, and permit an effective economic blockade.

While the Allies forbore to challenge him, however, Louis was free to sweep the Mediterranean with his privateers and cruisers and support his armies from the sea in their coastal advance into Piedmont and Catalonia. This was the crisis of the war. William was equal to the occasion. His instructions to Admiral Russell were a model for all time. Russell was to seek out the main French fleet and destroy it wherever it might be. If it had left Brest for the Mediterranean, he was to go in after it. The plan was practicable, moreover, for so long as Spain was undefeated, Cadiz and other useful ports were available as bases.

Accordingly, in July 1694 Russell led the English Grand Fleet on its first cruise into the Mediterranean. The results were prodigious. The French squadron off Barcelona disappeared into Toulon and the Catalonian campaign collapsed. France had no alternative but recourse to the policy that was ever afterwards to be her practice and her bane in conflict with Britain. Keeping her main fleet in being, she forced Britain to blockade it, and thereby ensured that the seas would lie open to her cruisers preying on British commerce. In this, as in every subsequent war, much British shipping was indeed destroyed. But that was because, by and large, only British and friendly commerce sailed the seas. French shipping was reduced to coastal traffic. By keeping the naval initiative Britain was able to enlarge her own economy to world-wide dimensions, while that of France was correspondingly restricted.

In 1694 the French expected Russell, having made his

demonstration, to retire home for a refit before the autumn storms made the journey dangerous. So, indeed, did Russell himself. Not so the King. Of his own responsibility William sent Russell the historic order to winter his fleet in Cadiz. Stores and artificers would be sent him there.

With grave doubts, Russell obeyed. All the next year a British fleet stayed in the Mediterranean and prevented any resumption of Louis's campaigns. Rich Levant and Italian convoys, Dutch and British, sailed in freedom. In desperation Louis bought off Savoy and forced Britain to withdraw her fleet to parry a threat of cross-Channel invasion. The result of the new strategy was military stalemate in the Mediterranean similar to that already reached in Flanders. The exhausted combatants making peace at Ryswick in 1697, French expansion was halted. But the death of the King of Spain being imminent, Louis now set himself to gain by the redistribution of Spanish territories more than all he had failed to get by war.

The prospect of a partition of the Spanish Empire on the death of the childless Charles II had exercised European diplomacy even before the accession of that sickly prince in 1665. The only alternative to partition, a Hapsburg reunion reviving the Empire of Charles V, was hardly thinkable in view of the opposition it would arouse. In partition itself immense issues were involved. Two of the principal claimants were the French Bourbons and the Austrian Hapsburgs. The gains of one would have to be balanced by gains to the other. In any case the Maritime Powers, Britain and Holland, would insist on compensation. The territories concerned were all of strategic or economic importance. Suppose the Spanish Netherlands or Spanish America came into French possession! Hardly less worrying was the disposition of the Mediterranean lands—the Balearic Islands, Ceuta, Oran, Naples, Sicily, Sardinia, the Tuscan ports and Lombardy. There was also the question of Spain herself.

In several plans put forward William showed his readiness to let Louis dominate Italy provided Spain were left in Hapsburg or non-Bourbon keeping. In such an event Spain and France would tend to be opposed, and the Maritime Powers would have the use of the Spanish ports, including Cadiz. William was even ready to admit a Bourbon in Madrid, provided the two crowns were kept separate and Britain were compensated. Compensation could take the form of the cession of the island of Minorca, with its superb harbour of Port Mahon, and either Gibraltar or Ceuta within the Straits.

As things turned out, Spanish patriotism reacted strongly against any idea of partition, and Charles on his deathbed made a will leaving all to Louis's grandson, Philip. This had the advantage that while Philip was not in the direct succession to the French throne yet Louis would be certain to support his claim with all the power of France. To ensure his concurrence, there was a rider offering everything to the Hapsburg Emperor's second son in case of his refusal. In the circumstances Louis can hardly be blamed for preferring this will to the treaty of partition he had recently signed with William. Indeed, at first, all except the Emperor were ready to accept the decision. William was far from satisfied, but so long as Parliament would not support him, he had to be content with the separation of the two crowns.

It was Louis who blundered. Far from keeping the kingdoms distinct, he showed every intention of uniting France, Spain and the Spanish Empire in a single exclusive economy. Nothing was more calculated to alarm the maritime nations. To the lax mercantilism of Old Spain, Britain saw succeeding an efficient and hostile autarky, which would lock out her cloth from some of its chief markets. Supporting this vast restrictive commercial system would be, moreover, an equally immense containing network of strategic power. Threatened with a France of these swollen dimensions, Britain pressed on with her own expansion towards commercial empire. The men who mattered in England in William's last years were men who fully understood the dependence of their way of life on the safety of their trade.

In September 1701 England, Holland and Austria signed the Treaty of the Grand Alliance. They agreed to recognize Philip in Spain and the Indies, provided the French and Spanish thrones were kept separate, and provided Austria were compensated in the Spanish Netherlands, Italy and the Balearics.

Britain would lose the use of Cadiz, but she could reckon on finding a good port open to her farther up the Mediterranean, since Port Mahon, Messina and Naples would all belong to an inland power without a navy.

Louis's recognition of the Pretender as James III now gave just the shock needed to unite William's factious British subjects behind the war effort. This combination of France and Spain was stronger than the Hapsburgs had been. It was more compact, fought on interior lines, and in the south imposed a barrier between Austria and the Maritime nations which only sea power could bridge. Fortunately, though Holland was weaker, Britain herself was stronger, with her thriving trade and industry, her confident finance, and her well-tried navy. This time, moreover, she had the experience of William's former successful strategy to guide her.

The opening move of the war, accordingly, was an attempt to get control of the Mediterranean. The first step was to find a base. The combined main fleets of Britain and Holland, with a strong military contingent, all under the command of Admiral Rooke, were detailed to seize Cadiz or Gibraltar. The attack on Cadiz, in August 1702, was carried out half-heartedly, and failed. But on his way home, the disgruntled admiral lit on an unexpected success in Vigo Bay. More important even than his destruction of the Indies *Flota* was the naval loss he inflicted. Ten French line-of-battle ships were taken, more were burnt. The fiasco at Cadiz was largely retrieved. Though Rooke did not open up the Mediterranean, he made its opening possible. For the Allies' prestige revived and Portugal shifted over into their camp.

By the Methuen Treaty concluded between England and Portugal in 1703 England took port in place of French claret, and Portugal increased her purchases of English cloth, much of which made its way on into Spain and even France. Vastly more important, however, was the free use of Lisbon as a base for Allied fleets, for it was this that made a Mediterranean strategy practicable. For this great advantage, unfortunately, a heavy price had to be paid. Requiring security on her land side, Portugal insisted on the Allies proclaiming the younger Austrian archduke as Charles III of Spain and sending substantial armies to the Peninsula. The price of a Mediterranean policy was a Peninsular War.

In the same year Sir Cloudesley Shovell convoyed the Levant trade through the Mediterranean and, making contact with the Duke of Savoy, encouraged him to abandon his French alliance. This was proof of the scope for Mediterranean action; and Marlborough, as William's heir in command and strategy, instantly perceived the opportunity to strike at France from the south in conjunction with Austria, Savoy and the rebel French Huguenots of the Cevennes.

Accordingly, in 1704, while Marlborough himself executed his march up the Rhine to save Vienna by the victory of Blenheim, Admiral Rooke led a powerful fleet into the Mediterranean to act on the coasts of Provence and Catalonia. The Savoyard ports of Nice and Villafranca controlled the coastal route into Italy and gave the duke contact with the fleet, whose presence in the Gulf of Lions cut France off from southern Italy. Catalonia had long been struggling like Portugal to free herself from the domination of Madrid, was the one region of Spain where Charles III was sure of a welcome and stood across the southern route between France and Spain. Toulon and Marseilles were also covered, the one the centre of French naval power, the other the principal breach in the Allies' loose blockade. They were the vulnerable centre of a slack French "underbelly" extending from the Upper Danube to the borders of Portugal.

For the moment, however, this Toulon Design was not to be. Savoy was fully occupied and Barcelona too resolutely defended. So when the fresh Brest fleet sailed past him into Toulon and Rooke was outnumbered, he fell back into the Straits, where he was joined by the Channel fleet under Shovell. Britain's fleets thus gathered together in readiness to strike or fend wherever the chief enemy concentration lay. But to be able to strike they had to have a nearer base than Lisbon. Cadiz being of ill omen, they decided to take Gibraltar.

The military aspect of Gibraltar is described in a later chapter. In the summer of 1704 the Rock was hardly better defended than it had been eighty years earlier. Adequately garrisoned it would have been difficult to approach from the land side, but it would still have lain open from the Bay and from the south. On 22 July 1704 the Prince of Hesse landed on the Isthmus from the east with 1,800 marines, while twenty-two sail of the line, English and Dutch, stood off the congested little town between the Old and New Moles. After a heavy bombardment and investment from the Isthmus and the water-front, the few hundred feeble defenders capitulated the next day. The attackers' only losses were about sixty killed, most of them in the accidental explosion of a powder magazine. This greatest of prizes was taken, however, for "Charles III", not for Queen Anne.

In Allied hands Gibraltar immediately assumed major strategic importance. It had been gained easily enough, but holding it was to be more difficult. The marines had to be reinforced and the battered defences somehow restored and strengthened before the Spanish could mount an attack from the Isthmus and the Toulon fleet could come up. Rooke had not finished taking on water at Tetuan when he got word of the enemy fleet's approach. He promptly stood out to sea in line of battle.

On 13 August 1704 the two great fleets met between Gibraltar and Malaga. Each was of more than fifty sail. Rooke had the weather gauge but Toulouse had got between him and Gibraltar. Short of ammunition and anxious for the ill-protected fortress, Rooke took no tactical risks. The fighting was heavy and casualties high. When night fell this "battle of the giants" was still undecided, but the British had only a few shots left per gun. All that night and the following day the French kept their position. But at dawn on the 15th when Rooke resolved to cut through to Gibraltar at any cost, he found the enemy gone. Unaware of his advantage, Toulouse had sailed back to Toulon.

The defence of Gibraltar by land that winter was of epic quality. Rooke, Byng and Shovell made their way home with the main fleet before the autumnal storms; but they left behind them a fourth great sailor, John Leake, with a winter squadron based on Lisbon to protect and carry succour to the garrison.

The Rock was weakest from the side of the Bay, where the bombardment had destroyed the defences. On the Isthmus front the new defenders speedily built batteries high on the Rock

(Willis's) and at the end of the Old Mole; these raked the trenches which the Spaniards pushed forward on the sands. A covered way, or palisaded sunk ditch "covered" by gunfire, effectively barred the way round the base of the Rock to the Old Mole. Two fortified lines supported by batteries blocked the way higher up along the slopes of scrub and loose rock which led to the Moorish Castle. These positions could not be greatly strengthened. The defenders, reduced by sickness and casualties, never numbered much above two thousand and the able German Prince of Hesse who commanded was at first ill-supported by his English subordinates.

During the seven months' siege the Spanish brought up over 12,000 men, and the French admiral, Pointis, landed a siege-train and several thousand French troops. But the winter weather, which the besiegers relied on to make relief impossible, proved the garrison's best ally. Leake twice arrived out of the storm with succour in the nick of time. Three main attempts were made on the fortress. The first was on 29 October 1704 when a goatherd led a forlorn hope of 500 men by dark up the pre-cipitous east face of the Rock to St. Michael's Cave. From this mountain ambush they were to concert with the fleet and the army in a combined assault. But that very day Leake's ships swept unexpectedly into the Bay, dispersing the French and landing marines who soon took the ambushers prisoner or forced them over the precipice. After this Leake stood by for a month, heartening the garrison by his presence, support-ing it with his marines and seamen, enfilading the Isthmus trenches with fire from his frigates. When he left again, it was only for a fortnight to fetch more stores and reinforcements which the Government had had carried to Lisbon.

The next attempt was by land alone on 7 February 1705. A surprise attack was launched in great strength directly across the rocky slopes. Both lines were forced, and the enemy got within a stone's throw of the Moorish Castle and victory when the self-sacrifice of a handful of marines saved precious minutes for support to come up. The attackers faltered, and fell back across the lines they had just won. But the margin of safety had been small.

The last attempt was to have been by sea as well as by land.

C

But the rains which for months had drenched and sickened the Spanish in their trenches now turned to tempest and Pointis's squadron dared not stand into the Bay. Leake, however, came round again from Lisbon and on 21 March burst upon them a second time out of the storm. Five great ships were taken or destroyed and the rest fled to Toulon. There was no further attempt. The "symbol of Mediterranean lordship" had once again passed from the Spaniard into alien hands.

This victory in the Mediterranean following that on the Danube put the Allies in the ascendant. Nevertheless the capture of Gibraltar was not all gain, for it involved Britain more deeply in the Peninsula. Marlborough and the Government now unwisely pledged themselves to the war aim of "No Peace without Spain", meaning that the Hapsburgs must first be restored there. This determination was in turn reinforced by a first-fruit of the Mediterranean success, the capture of Barcelona, the capital city of Catalonia.

In midsummer 1705 a strong Allied fleet again entered the Mediterranean under Sir Cloudesley Shovell. It had some 8,000 troops on board, together with "Charles III", the Prince of Hesse, and the eccentric Earl of Peterborough, who was in chief command. Charles managing to divert the expedition to Catalonia rather than the Riviera, it drew up in Barcelona roads. Here precious weeks were slipping by when a snap decision of Peterborough's changed the situation. On 13 September a small picked contingent under Peterborough and Hesse set off late from the camp at the east of the town as if going to Tarragona. Before dawn on the 14th, however, gunfire was heard from the citadel of Monjuich to the west. This was rushed; lost again, when Hesse was killed; then recovered by Peterborough, whose blind fury stopped the panic; and finally it was held. The city surrendered and soon all the east coast rose on behalf of Charles. There was already an army on the Portuguese frontier. With Madrid thus threatened from the Ebro as well as the Tagus, the prospect in Spain seemed bright for the spring of 1706, the more so by contrast with Allied checks in Flanders and Italy.

The results of the year 1706 were, however, the reverse of

what might have been expected. Victorious in Flanders and Italy, the Allies were all but driven out of Spain. In the spring, while the Allied fleet was away refitting in Lisbon, French land forces besieged Barcelona and a squadron from Toulon held the coast. Charles defended the city stoutly, but it was on the point of collapse when Leake arrived characteristically out of the blue. Thereupon Bourbon resistance gave way everywhere, and Galway's army pushed on out of Portugal to occupy Madrid. This was Charles's opportunity. But he threw it away by interminable delays in Catalonia. By the time he joined Galway Spanish patriotism had turned decidedly against the heretical foreigner in favour of Philip, and the Allies had no alternative but to retire on Valencia and the fleet. A great chance had been lost. Few realized, unfortunately, that it could hardly come again.

The trouble lay in the very success of sea power, which encouraged illusory hopes and policies. It was everywhere victorious. The Toulon fleet had not ventured out. Apart from Minorca, all the Balearics had fallen to it. The Barbary States were quiescent and trade was being reopened enthusiastically with Italy and the Levant. The Spanish east coast lay open. As the conquest of Spain had been made a war aim, it was not easy, in these circumstances, to remember that the real enemy was still France. In fact, by the end of 1706 the Allies had achieved nearly all their original objectives. Though the war was to go on for six more years, they had won, except for Minorca, as much as they were ever to get. What led Britain to overvalue the Spanish affair still more, perhaps, was the fact that she did not yet have a base nearer Toulon than Lisbon in which to winter and refit a fleet. Gibraltar was too distant and inadequate. Until such a base had been gained the fullest expression of sea power would be denied.

Marlborough's plans for 1707 took account of this naval deficiency. In his Great Design he proposed to execute the long-contemplated assault on Toulon from Italy and from the sea. This was to be followed up by a two-fold invasion of France, from the south, led by Prince Eugene and supported by the fleet, and from the north-west under his own direction. The base of operations was to be, once it was taken, Toulon itself.

But the Allies had achieved so many of their aims already that, as is the way with victors, their counsels grew divided. Refused possession of Flanders, which Marlborough had conquered, the new Emperor Joseph determined to make certain of Milan and Naples, though these had actually been promised to his brother Charles. In March 1707 he made a separate treaty with Louis neutralizing Italy, thus allowing the French to transfer their forces from Italy to other fronts, including Spain.

The first result of divided counsels was consequently a further setback in Spain. From the base at Valencia Charles once more shirked his opportunity and marched his Spaniards north to secure Catalonia, leaving Galway with the Portuguese and British to make the direct attempt on Madrid. Met by Marlborough's brilliant Jacobite nephew, the Duke of Berwick, in superior strength on the broad plain of Murcia, Galway was routed at Almanza in April 1707. He barely extricated a regiment or two to resume contact with the fleet and save the coastal fortresses.

A more serious result was to enfeeble the attempt on Toulon. It was not till the end of June that Eugene crossed the Var and began to push his way along the coast to the outskirts of Toulon. Though stoutly supported by Shovell's ships, he made slow progress, and the French had time to reinforce their positions. A determined assault might even at the end of July have carried the town. But Eugene's heart was not in an enterprise the naval side of which he did not understand. In the third week of August he raised the siege and retired into Italy.

Shovell was furious. His fleet had supplied the food, the stores and guns, his country was paying the men. Lost in a storm on his way back to England, he never learnt the extent of his success. On his approach the French had sunk their ships at their shallow moorings to save them from capture or burning, and most of them could never be raised again. The French navy did not recover from this self-inflicted wound.

Though this Great Design broke down thus miserably, it had eased the position in Catalonia, where some gains were made. Even these would be lost, however, unless the fleet could winter nearer the scene of operations. In 1708 General James

Stanhope was appointed to the command of the English in Spain. As Toulon could not be taken, both he and Marlborough were convinced of the need to secure Minorca, whose harbour of Mahon had been one of King William's objectives. Admiral Leake was now in command of the fleet. He had bombarded Cagliari and obtained Sardinian grain for Charles's Spanish armies. His latest orders were to chastise the Pope for an unfriendly Jacobitist gesture. But on word from Stanhope, Leake laid everything aside and took his fleet over to Minorca.

The first British conquest of Minorca followed a pattern which became very familiar before the century ended. While Leake kept the seas clear, Stanhope left Barcelona with 1,700 men on 3 September 1708, picked up more at Majorca on the 8th, and six days later began landings on the island. While ships of the squadron took possession of Ciudadella and Fornelles, both good fortified harbours, Stanhope occupied the town of Mahon at the head of its famous bay. The garrison retired into the splendid Fort St. Philip on its promontory controlling the narrow harbour mouth. Until it had been taken the port would be useless. There being no roads cannon were landed by the sailors just out of range of the fort, and mounted in batteries under fire. A preliminary bombardment followed by the storming of the outworks proved enough. On 30 September, 1708 the fortress yielded. Although the island was taken in the name of "King Charles" and received a Carlist governor, Stanhope put an English garrison in the fort. Charles refused every inducement to cede this important part of his "inheritance"; but Britain remained in occupation until his rival Philip confirmed her status there at Utrecht in 1713.

This great success, regarded at the time as giving Britain the dominion of the Mediterranean, unhappily contributed to harden the Allies' hearts over Spain. Not content with insisting that Louis recognize Charles as King of Spain, the Whigs expected him to help enforce these terms against his own grandson. It was too much for Louis, too much for the French and Spanish peoples. They fought on more valiantly than ever.

In 1709, the year of these negotiations, the Allies lost more ground in Spain. But the next year, reinforced from Italy and inspired by Stanhope, they opened a vigorous offensive. After two costly victories Charles and Stanhope pushed up the Ebro to Saragossa and thence across to Madrid itself. But their triumph was again short-lived. Instead of being joined by the army of Portugal, they found Marshal Vendôme on that side with 10,000 horse. Outnumbered and destitute of supplies, their communications exposed to the pitiless Spanish guerrillas, in the middle of November they began their retreat to the coast. On 9 December Stanhope, surrounded in the streets of Brihuega, surrendered with 4,000 British troops. Though the Carlist army escaped to Barcelona, after this catastrophe the Allies were at last disillusioned.

It was pointless to continue fighting. The fall of the Whigs the same year and the death of the Emperor Joseph in April 1711 leaving Charles his heir brought the war to an end. To support Charles now in Spain and the Indies would have been to abet a Hapsburg preponderance as dangerous as the Bourbon. In 1711 the Tory Government, ignoring Britain's obligations to her allies, agreed with France on the terms of a separate peace, broadly identical with those originally laid down in the Grand Alliance. Their principal ally having gone over to the enemy, the Dutch and Germans soon had to follow suit, and a general peace was arranged at Utrecht during 1712-13.

By anticipating her allies Britain secured advantages for herself which she would hardly have obtained at a general conference, although they corresponded to the part her fleet, her subsidies and her army had played in the war. Besides security in Flanders and gains in America, she was confirmed in her place, won during the war, as the dominant Mediterranean power. The extent of her gains can best be seen by comparing the position in 1713 with that a century before.

In the Eastern Mediterranean Turkey had now passed her zenith. Though not greatly reduced territorially, she was weakened by internal decay and the pressure on her frontiers now not only of the Hapsburgs but of the new Russian state and the vigorous Maritime Powers. The prosperity of Britain's Levant Company was now at its peak, though Dutch rivalry was still keen and the Marseilles merchants would begin to pick up with the return of peace. By 1713 the West's commercial thrust had more than offset its strategic loss of the island of Crete. It was supported, moreover, by the growing independence shown by the Barbary states towards the Porte and their increasing deference to the navies and trade interests of the sea powers.

In the central Mediterranean equally important changes had taken place. The Knights of Malta were no longer fighting for existence, but were raising their splendid palaces and hospitals. Venice was declining alike from military exhaustion and the commercial competition. Of the smaller states of Italy, Savoy was given Sicily, and with this island and the Riviera ports of Nice and Villafranca seemed destined for a maritime career. Trade interest and the pressure from either side of Austria and France encouraged her to keep the friendship of Britain. Much the same was also true of Tuscany, whose free port of Leghorn continued to prosper.

In the Western Mediterranean as a whole a favourable new equilibrium had appeared, an equilibrium that was to be the basis of British policy from that day to this. Thus France had been excluded from Italy under Louis XIV as she had been under Mazarin. The large part previously enjoyed by the Marseilles merchants in the trade of the Levant, Barbary and Italy had been taken away by Dutch and British supremacy at sea. While the Dutch, in their turn, had been so exhausted by their effort on land that, however their trade might flourish in the future, they could hardly again hope to rival Britain in a show of power. Similarly, the united Hapsburg domination of Italy had been removed by the death of Charles II of Spain. Being Bourbon and maritime, Spain was given no place in the new Italy. Of her former territories Sicily went to Savoy, while Naples, Sardinia and Lombardy passed to the surviving Austrian Hapsburg. Having as yet neither fleets nor trade pretensions, the Emperor and the Duke might be relied on as inveterate anti-Bourbons and allies of Britain. In their hands Naples and Sicily offered facilities for supply and refit complementary to Minorca, increased British political influence, and gave additional protection to the Levant trade.

Around the Iberian Peninsula, finally, Britain now possessed in Portuguese Lisbon and her own Gibraltar and Port Mahon a system of overseas naval bases unmatched anywhere by other powers. Peninsular nations like France and Spain saw these new bases extending ominously from the old ones at Chatham, Portsmouth and Plymouth to encircle them completely. Now that Britain was also confirmed in her alliance with the German Emperor, the Dutch and the Portuguese, this system even extended to the land frontiers of France and Spain. Though the means by which the peace had been obtained were at first resented by Austria and Holland, after 1714 the Hanoverian Succession and the Whig ascendancy removed this bitterness and completed Britain's triumph.

CHAPTER III

INFLUENCE OF SEA POWER, 1713-83

(a) 1713-48

BRITAIN had thus gained spectacularly from the system of alliances and the Mediterranean strategy laid down by William III and developed by Marlborough. The events of the succeeding seventy years were to show that she would depart from this "Old System" at her peril. Broadly speaking, down to 1748 Britain tried to hold her position in the Mediterranean and in the world upon these principles and in the face of resolute opposition from the French and Spanish who felt, justifiably, that they had been outwitted. But having gained all that she could hope to gain by these methods Britain saw herself grudgingly subserving the interests of allies on the Continent just when she was most anxious to extend her ambitions still farther into the New World. Her reaction to this situation was the policy accepted in the Seven Years War.

Accordingly, between 1756 and 1763 Britain threw over her former allies in favour of Frederick of Prussia, in effect neutralized the Mediterranean, and put her supreme effort into the colonial and maritime war. The immediate reward was triumph undreamed of, dominion over North America and India and unchallenged supremacy at sea. In the longer run, however, this policy proved mistaken. It lost Britain her allies, the powers of Europe being still too great to be thus cavalierly ignored by a nation so closely bound to them territorially and economically. And it lost her most of America. It was to be the achievement of the Younger Pitt to pull his country back into the European states system and by concentrating her effort at the centre of power to redirect her strategy into the Mediterranean and by way of the Mediterranean to India. The result then, was a return to the policies of William and Marlborough and a triumph even greater than that won in their day.

Down to the middle 1730s Britain succeeded in maintaining her trade and power in the Mediterranean, though the forces reconciled by treaty in 1713 were by no means joined in any stable equilibrium. Britain, indeed, was the only satisfied power. The chief threat to the *status quo*, in the West at any rate, was the rivalry of Spain and Austria in Italy. Any advantage allowed to the one would be certain to drive the other into the camp of France and stimulate French revival.

The Emperor Charles VI remained unwilling to recognize Philip as King of Spain and resented the separation of Sicily from Naples. For his part, Philip kept urging Britain to return Gibraltar; while his second wife, the Parmesan Elizabeth Farnese, vigorously pressed Spanish claims in Italy in order to procure an inheritance for her sons by him. In support of her ambitions she raised up a Parmese priest named Alberoni as chief minister of Spain. Within a year or two of the peace the dockyards of Spain were humming with unusual life, and it was clear that a new Italian settlement would soon have to be arranged.

From these developments Britain could not stand aloof. Between 1714 and 1721 her diplomacy was guided by General Stanhope, the conqueror of Minorca. As co-author of the Triple Alliance (1716) he had already begun the consolidation of the peace by allying Britain and Holland with France, now ruled by the Regent Orleans. He hoped to extend this system by bringing in the Hapsburgs and the Spanish Bourbons, but this could only be done by revising the Italian settlement. He proposed, therefore, to transfer Sicily from Savoy to the Emperor and guarantee his other gains in the Netherlands and Lombardy, on condition Charles gave up his claim to the Spanish throne and accepted Don Carlos, Elizabeth's son, as heir to Parma. Savoy would have to be content with Sardinia instead of Sicily, but British Mediterranean interests need not be affected.

Neither party was much pleased. Believing Stanhope partial to Austria Philip decided to forestall any move by the Emperor. In July 1717 a great fleet sailed from Barcelona and landed troops in Sardinia. Stanhope thereupon advised Charles to offer Tuscany as well as Parma. Charles accepting these terms in principle in May 1718, Admiral Sir George Byng was sent off to the Mediterranean with twenty sail of the line and instructions to give effect to the new arrangements. On his way he was to warn the Spanish government that he would oppose any further landings in Sicily or Italy.

In June 1718 Alberoni dispatched a still greater armada, this time for Sicily; and simultaneously a chain of intrigue circled the European capitals aiming to overthrow the Hanoverians in England and the Regency in France. Byng delivered his warning, but Alberoni only bade him go ahead. He reached Naples on 1 August to find that Sicily had already fallen to the Marquis of Lede. It was for the fleet now to retrieve the situation. On the 9th Byng sighted the Spanish fleet and the flying victory off Cape Passaro followed. The effect was decisive. De Lede's army being cut off, the Austrians were free to reduce the island at leisure. A blow had been struck at the reviving Spanish navy and at its guiding spirit. Confronted by the united forces of Britain and France, Philip had to sacrifice Alberoni, and in February 1720 he acceded to the Quadruple Alliance. By this vigorous assertion of sea power, Britain thus kept the south of Italy in trustworthy hands and averted the Bourbon-Jacobite danger.

Checked in Italy, Spain next gave her attention to the Gibraltar grievance. Alike from the point of view of honour, trade and national security the retention of Gibraltar by a foreign and Protestant power was hard for Spaniards to accept. In this they had the sympathy of Stanhope and other British ministers who fully appreciated what an obstacle the fortress presented to the good relations they wanted with Spain. Indeed, a clause of the treaty seemed to imply a temporary tenure only; whenever Britain should give up Gibraltar Spain was to be offered the first refusal.

In 1718, before the news of Byng's victory, Stanhope had offered to return the fortress conditionally, but Alberoni rejected the bait. In 1720 the French Regent, without authority, renewed this offer in order to get Philip to accept the Italian settlement. Though Philip joined the Quadruple Alliance without express reserve, it was nevertheless in the belief that Britain was ready to give up Gibraltar in return for trade concessions he was granting.

However, all parties were reckoning without the British public. No sooner was cession rumoured than a general outcry was excited, and ministers had to give private assurances that no such step would be contemplated. The traders must have been behind this, for Gibraltar was as yet no place to touch the nation's heart.

Philip now brought pressure to bear. The trade concessions were suspended, the garrison's supplies cut off, complaints lodged at the presence of Moors and Jews in the town contrary to the Treaty of Utrecht. A concentration of troops at Cadiz and Algeciras seemed so ominous to the British Government, that Byng's fleet was rushed out and Brigadier Kane brought reinforcements from Minorca.

British fears were increased by evidence that France and Spain were drawing together. A marriage alliance was in prospect and French influence was to be used to get Gibraltar restored. To meet this crisis Stanhope's successor, Carteret, astutely persuaded George I to promise to return Gibraltar on the "first favourable opportunity to regulate this article with consent of parliament". In view of the recent attitude of the Commons this could only have been a ruse to postpone a decision indefinitely. Philip pretended to be content. By the Treaty of Madrid in June 1721 mutual guarantees were exchanged and a common front proposed for the forthcoming European Congress at Cambrai. In the same treaty was incorporated a renewal of the 1667 Commercial Treaty as amended by recent trade agreements.

When the Congress met Spain and Austria soon saw that their separate aims would never be admitted by the mediating powers. The Emperor now wanted, in addition, an international guarantee of the female succession in all his hereditary dominions—the so-called Pragmatic Sanction—and the withdrawal of Dutch and British opposition to his Ostend Company for trading to the Indies. Philip was depressed by his failure to recover Gibraltar, and when in March 1725 the French broke off their marriage agreement he decided to retaliate.

Six weeks after the return of the Infanta France and Britain were surprised to find the supposed inveterate enemies, Charles and Philip, in close alliance and pledged to advance each other's claims. An ultimatum to Britain to restore Gibraltar on pain of forfeiting the trade concessions was followed in November 1725 by the Treaty of Vienna, by which Austria promised to help Spain recover Gibraltar in return for Spain's admitting the Ostend Company to her overseas trade. This represented a combination of land and sea power potentially as menacing as that which had faced William III, and called for an equally resolute reply.

Britain hurriedly constructed the Alliance of Hanover, a new Grand Alliance, only with the roles of France and Austria reversed. Fleets were sent to the West Indies and paraded the coasts of Spain. Kane again took command at Gibraltar. As a result neither Vienna power was able to move at sea. The subsidies that the Emperor needed could not be paid as Philip's *flota* could not sail, and Philip found himself without money and condemned to action on his own. That autumn when the Mediterranean fleet returned to England in the usual way a squadron was left behind to winter in the bay of Gibraltar.

Philip had now only one resource left, and he laid siege to the fortress. Kane having been ordered to avoid provocation, the small garrison looked on while the Spanish advanced their lines under its guns. Happily, just before hostilities began on 11 February 1727, Sir Charles Wager arrived with reinforcements and stores which nearly doubled its strength. The fleet's presence, moreover, enabled supplies to be got in from Barbary and Minorca. Still, when Kane left on 23 February, Brigadier Clayton had only 3,000 men to hold back the 20,000 of the Count de las Torres.

This siege lasted some four months. The Spanish batteries on the Isthmus destroyed the Old Mole and much of the northwest corner of the town. The conversion of the morass into a lake had narrowed the direct approach from the west, but the Spanish had no difficulty getting close under the rock face so that the British guns could not bear on them. Once there they started mining operations to blow up the batteries overhead. The ships of the fleet were a great help, however, dispersing Spanish craft and enfilading the enemy trenches from both sides of the Isthmus. Being so exposed, the besiegers lost heavily from gunfire and sickness and a great many deserted into the

Rock. There was no direct assault and British casualties—some 300 killed and wounded—were due as much to their own gun-bursts as to enemy cannon.

In June word arrived that peace had been signed in Paris on 31 May between the Emperor and the Allies. So a nine months truce was agreed upon. However, Philip made no move to shift his army and the land blockade continued until March 1728 when, by the Convention of the Pardo, Spain agreed to attend a Congress at Soissons.

But again at this Congress discussion of Gibraltar was ruled out by Britain because of Parliament's stubbornness. Unable to satisfy her husband's ambition, Elizabeth Farnese once more turned to her own and promptly deserted the Emperor. In November 1729 by the Treaty of Seville she admitted all the demands of Britain and France, including a resumption of the commercial treaties and silence over Gibraltar. All she asked in return, it appeared, was their backing in Parma and Tuscany.

The Emperor continued defiant, however, until the ascendancy of Walpole in the British Cabinet opened a fresh approach. By another treaty of Vienna, in March 1731, the special objects of both Emperor and Queen were secured. In return for Britain's guarantee of the Pragmatic Sanction the Emperor agreed to admit Spanish garrisons in Parma and Tuscany and suppress the Ostend Company. Six months later Europe was treated to the spectacle of an Anglo-Spanish fleet escorting Spanish troops to Leghorn. Walpole was well content with the renewal of the trade treaties and the prospect of peace. He was not aware that a condition of Philip's acceptance of the earlier Treaty of Seville had been a secret clause by which Bourbon reunion was foreshadowed and France's good offices promised for the restoration of Gibraltar.

Walpole's success was, indeed, illusory. His initiative had been a snub to his French ally and from that time forward the great French minister Fleury worked steadily to restore his country's power and independence. The question of the Polish Succession which distracted Europe down to 1738 gave him his opportunity. While Walpole's pacific isolationism led him to disregard the obligation just incurred to help the Emperor and thus prejudiced the "Old Alliance", Fleury's adroit diplomacy transformed the place of France in Europe. On land she was strengthened by the acquisition of Lorraine. Diplomatically she was secured by the Bourbon Family Compact of 1733 with Spain. Even in the Mediterranean the development of the Spanish Queen's ambitions worked to French advantage. Don Carlos no longer ruled in Tuscany where he had been relatively innocuous, but ruled instead in Naples and Sicily. No less serious was the decline of British trade with Spain, Italy and the Levant, especially as British wares were being pushed out of those markets by the thriving commerce of Marseilles. When Britain at last roused herself to defend her interests she reckoned on war with France as inevitably as with Spain. It was the only means left of recovering the ground lost by this feeble diplomacy.

Nevertheless, it was with Spain that hostilities first occurred. Another reforming minister, Patiño, tightening up the Spanish imperial economy, provoked the friction with West Indian smugglers that led to the War of Jenkins's Ear. His reforms were equally felt by British merchants trading to Old Spain; while the recapture of Oran in 1732 suggested a forward policy in North Africa which, in conjunction with the Family Compact and the settlement of Don Carlos in Naples, threatened Britain's Mediterranean power.

The nation's instinctive awareness of these issues forced Walpole in the summer of 1738 to reinforce the small frigate squadron centred on Gibraltar, and demand reparation. But the arrangement come to in January 1739 by the Convention of the Pardo did not satisfy the merchant interest. Admiral Haddock's ships were duly recalled in terms of the agreement, but in March the orders were revoked by the Duke of Newcastle, his finger as always on the pulse of the electorate. Spain's attitude stiffening, in June 1739 Haddock was instructed to begin reprisals.

The opening moves were made in the West Indies where Spain was thought most vulnerable. Britain's Mediterranean effort was limited to trade protection, watching Cadiz and Cartagena, and guarding Minorca against surprise. But on the Emperor's death and the invasion of Silesia by Frederick of Prussia in December 1740 the Spanish War merged into that of the Austrian Succession, Britain regained her old ally, and the Mediterranean resumed its strategic importance. Elizabeth Farnese lost no time in claiming the rest of the Italian inheritance, Lombardy, for her second son, Don Philip, who had recently married a French princess. To effect this design she proposed a three-fold advance on Milan. While one army was to be landed in the Tuscan ports another, with French goodwill, was to be infiltrated through the Western Alps or along the Riviera. Together they were to link up with a third army brought up from Naples through the Papal territories. The Empress, Maria Theresa, being fully occupied with Frederick in Silesia, the outcome of this Italian war depended on the British fleet and on the attitude of Charles Emmanuel of Savoy, whose dominions barred the land routes into Lombardy.

Much under strength and distracted by the needs of commerce protection, the fleet failed in its main task. In the winter of 1741-2, while Don Philip occupied Savoy, a French squadron covered the passage of Spanish transports from Cadiz to Tuscany. Nevertheless a threat of naval bombardment sufficed to keep Naples and Genoa neutral and so spoilt part of the Spanish plan. The fall of Walpole, moreover, early in 1742, enabled his successor Carteret to give British policy more of a continental bias. The Mediterranean fleet was reinforced and Charles Emmanuel, thus encouraged and bribed with a share of the Austrian subsidy, joined Britain and Austria in the Treaty of Worms (September 1743). This promised him Sicily and the Genoese port of Finale, a return to the idea of a maritime Savoy. No sooner was the barrier against Spain thus strengthened, however, than France decided to enter the war as a principal. As at the same time Frederick resumed hostilities in Germany, the Empress was still at a disadvantage.

The Sardinian alliance gave the fleet a forward base at Villafranca from which it could assist the allied armies; but there was little Haddock's successor, Admiral Matthews, could do until the Toulon fleet had been dealt with. His opportunity came in February 1744 when the combined fleets of France and Spain pushed out of Toulon to challenge his worn, foul ships at their station off Hyères. But the long action was drawn. It was a grave disappointment for Britain, and the admiral was court-martialled. Fortunately France now fell back on her defeatist technique of mere commerce destruction, breaking up her fleet into small raiding squadrons. British trade suffered heavily and the fleet's supply problem grew acute. But the French navy did not again participate directly in the Italian war and French trade also suffered heavily from the attacks of British cruisers and of privateers such as the amazing Fortunatus Wright.

The next two years were very difficult. Rowley, taking over from Matthews, had to withdraw his main fleet to Mahon to refit, and thereafter, on instructions from home, to cover Cartagena and Cadiz. For the French, by shifting their weight towards the Atlantic, increased the fear of a Jacobite invasion of England, and thereby drew off British strength from the Riviera. Villafranca was lost. The French and Spanish armies, joined in May 1745 by the previously hesitant Genoese, were able to resume their coastal advance and transform the Italian scene. There came the long-delayed thrust from Naples round upon Genoa, and after three and a half years the junction of the Spanish armies was achieved. By the late autumn Milan and the line of the Po were in Spanish hands and Charles Emmanuel was making overtures of peace.

Yet the enemy's very success proved his undoing. His extended communications were particularly vulnerable from the sea, and Rowley's successor, Medley, took a heavy toll of Spanish transports on both shores of the peninsula. In the crisis the Empress again made terms with Frederick so as to be able to reinforce Lombardy early in 1746. Moreover, elated by victory, the Spanish Queen deflected her armies towards her cherished Parma.

So again fortune turned. Charles Emmanuel thought better of his defection and fell upon the unsuspecting French garrisons. Incited by the Duke of Newcastle, upon whose fleets and subsidies they were so dependent, the allies found themselves launching a campaign through Provence towards Toulon in a manner reminiscent of Marlborough's Design. But for an unsuccessful diversion to win Corsica for the Sardinian king Medley might have harried the enemy's retreat to the point of collapse. It was not to be. Eugene's experience was repeated.

D

Maria Theresa was too anxious to recover Naples, Charles
Emmanuel to get Finale, to force the campaign home. Reinforcements arrived from Flanders and Catalonia to stiffen the resistance around Cannes and Antibes, and the Genoese rose in the
allies' rear. By the spring of 1747 they had been thrust back
across the Var.

In 1747 the British Government, sensing the stalemate in
the Mediterranean, ordered a reduction there to provide
reinforcements for India, where Madras had been lost. Naval
operations were confined to the siege of Genoa. In April the
following year Britain and France arranged preliminaries of
peace at Aix-la-Chapelle.

Negotiations had been going on for two years, reflecting the
changing fortunes of the war. The accession of the pacific
Ferdinand VI in 1746 and the strong mercantile interest in a
resumption of trade with Spain led to hopes of separating that
country from France. Several ministers would willingly have
given up Gibraltar to ensure Spanish goodwill, though no one
thought of parting with Minorca, for its importance as a repair
base had been obvious and it dominated Toulon. But it was the
Duke of Newcastle who had charge of the final negotiation and
to him the surrender of Gibraltar was unthinkable. His chief
concern was to cement the traditional alliance with Austria
and Holland, but here French diplomacy was too clever for
him. Conditions everywhere made for stalemate and consequent
discontent. British victories at sea and in America and the
exhaustion of France from the blockade had been largely offset
by failure in India, the collapse of the Low Countries and allied
bankruptcy. So Britain ended the war as she had begun it
without any real friends. The nearest, after all, was Spain
which, under its new ruler, seemed ready to forgive or at least
forget.

This general frustration was reflected in the Italian settlement. By denying Charles Emmanuel the gains promised him at
Worms Britain secured Maria Theresa's grudging acquiescence
in the award of Parma to Don Philip. Don Carlos was confirmed
in the Two Sicilies. Thus there was no alleviation for either
Britain or Austria and the King of Sardinia had to forgo his
maritime dreams. If the King felt thwarted by these arrange-

ments, the Empress affected to believe she had suffered nothing but loss. She did not care to admit how much she had been enabled in difficult circumstances to keep.

The growing estrangement of Austria meant a corresponding decline in British influence in the Mediterranean. The result of the long struggle, therefore, was to confirm the decay of British Mediterranean power and revive that of France and Spain to a position more in keeping with their geography and national instinct. The course of the war suggested, moreover, that so long as France divided her effort between Europe and overseas, Britain had no need to act decisively in the Mediterranean. In any case, her interests were already shifting across the Atlantic.

(b) 1748-83

Except in the Mediterranean the Peace of Aix was never more than a truce, but there the essence of a settlement did emerge. Ferdinand VI of Spain was anxious to revive trade with Britain, while in London and Madrid the respective ambassadors, Ricardo Wall and Benjamin Keene, strove hard for a permanent friendship. Keene's Commercial Treaty of 1750 cancelled the obnoxious Asiento clause and restored the 1667 tariff. At Gibraltar General Bland put down the smuggling and co-operated happily with his neighbours at Algeçiras and San Roque. British ministers believed that a conciliatory approach might detach Spain from the Bourbon Compact. The Spanish hoped that Gibraltar and Minorca, withheld from them as enemies, might be returned to them as friends.

From Minorca Britain kept a watchful eye on French activity in Italy and the Levant. Though her government was slow to recognize the fact, she was now friendless in the Italian world. By the Treaty of Aranjuez of 1752 Italian dynastic squabbles were ended, Spain joining with Austria in a mutual territorial guarantee, to which Sardinia and Parma later acceded. Into this closed system Britain and France were both anxious to break, but the advantage lay with France since the Austrian Chancellor, Kaunitz, was her unacknowledged ally. Kaunitz was determined to free the Hapsburgs from their dependence on

Britain. For him the enemy was Prussia, and against her Britain was obviously less serviceable than France. There being no outstanding Italian issue for the British fleet to influence, the way was eased for the realignment of the powers in the Diplomatic Revolution of 1756, when Frederick and Maria Theresa hastily exchanged their partners. Before this happened, however, Britain and France were already at war not only overseas, where hostilities had never really ceased, but in the Mediterranean as well.

So far as Britain was concerned the Seven Years War (1756-63), unlike its predecessors, was a struggle for supremacy outside Europe. The continental war was only a subsidiary interest important because it divided France's energies. The initial loss of Minorca symbolizes this change of emphasis, for it was the impatient and bungled American opening that left the home front weakened against invasion and made it impossible to reinforce the Mediterranean in time.

For the relief of Minorca the Government chose Admiral John Byng, but allowed him few ships and those poor and undermanned. On reaching Gibraltar he learnt that, except for St. Philip's Castle, the island was already in French hands. Landing on 18 April at Ciudadella at the opposite end from Mahon, the French had been warmly received by the Minorquins, and the outlying British detachments had had to retire hastily inside the fortress leaving the great harbour and naval works undefended. Against Richelieu's 15,000 men the garrison mustered only 3,000, not enough to man the enormous walls. In the inexcusable absence of the governor, Lord Tyrawley, the gouty and normally bed-ridden General Blakeney, eighty-four years of age, had to bear the entire burden of command.

Blakeney was still blithely holding out when Byng's arrival on 19 May cut off the French from home. If Byng had had a head for strategy he would have seen that by merely keeping his own fleet in being he could have so imperilled the whole French enterprise that their fleet would have been obliged to attack his under a tactical disadvantage. Instead he chose to force the issue.

The battle began with a race for the weather gauge. This the British won after an hour's crowded sailing, only to be thwarted by ineffective signalling which led to several vessels of the van being disabled by accurate French fire aloft. Meanwhile Byng and the rear ships were held back by the damage to those ahead in their division, and the French Admiral, Galissonière, had he been intent on a decision, might have cut in between and smashed the crippled British van. After five hours the action ended with the French making off in the dark to put themselves between the British and St. Philip's Castle.

The next step was the fateful council of war of 24 May 1756. Not appreciating the cards he held, Byng put the inappropriate questions: Would an attack on the French fleet give any prospect of relieving Minorca? Would Gibraltar be endangered by an accident to the fleet? The answers were inevitable.

It was some weeks before Richelieu could believe that the English had really gone. Reinforcements reaching him, on 28 June the garrison surrendered. After seventy days' siege and three weeks' steady bombardment or assault, it was worn out with the ceaseless duty in the steamy underground chambers. The terms were generous. Subsequently Blakeney was made an Irish peer and received the Order of the Bath. But the Government's responsibility could not be so lightly shelved, and there followed the court-martial and execution of the unfortunate Byng.

The loss of Minorca, the fall of Oswego in America, and the sudden opening of the continental war by his new ally, Frederick, combined to bring down Newcastle's government. His "Old System" was dead. But although the Duke had not realized it a more immediately profitable system was being born. Minorca gone, the Mediterranean could no longer serve as the traditional pincer. But with Austria hostile, it was less important that it should. None of the Italian states, least of all Sardinia, would now risk attachment to the British cause. The rise to power of Pitt in November 1756 foreshadowed the changing order. With Frederick's whole-hearted approval, Britain was to "put herself on board her fleet" and force France to attempt to win America in Germany.

Before taking this decision Pitt made one more effort to reconcile the Old System with the new situation by breaking down the Aranjuez agreements. He offered to guarantee Naples to Don Carlos's family when that prince should succeed Ferdinand in Madrid. To Charles Emmanuel of Sardinia he offered compensation in that event. To Ferdinand himself he offered Gibraltar back in return for help in recovering Minorca. It was a splendid bait, possibly inspired by a parallel French offer of Minorca. But Ferdinand refused to be drawn.

If this Gibraltar offer seems unlike the great Pitt, it must be remembered that he was following in the wake of Stanhope, that the times were desperate and the stakes high. So far, Gibraltar had by no means demonstrated its value, even for commerce, to be set against the advantages of a Spanish alliance. What Britain gained, moreover, France would lose. Pitt was closer than we are to the traditions of Anglo-Spanish friendship. He was no doubt also influenced by Lord Tyrawley's account of the "fatherless and motherless defenceless state" the fortress was reduced to, its uselessness for docking, and the high cost of putting such defects right.

Within the Mediterranean no change of strategy was at first apparent, beyond that imposed by the loss of the base that had covered Toulon. Hawke, succeeding Byng, stood off Toulon as long as he could and when winter recalled him left Saunders at Gibraltar with five ships. But these were too foul, in April the next year, to stop an equal squadron from Toulon escaping to America with relief for Louisburg. British trade suffered from French and Barbary cruisers and the French quietly occupied Corsica, under an arrangement with Genoa, to complete their strategic triangle, Toulon, Mahon and St. Florent.

For the next two years it was Admiral Osborne's task to prevent superior French forces from escaping through the Gut with further relief for Louisburg. Operating chiefly from Gibraltar he effected a series of remarkable interceptions. On 28 February 1758 he won a victory while watching Cartagena, where a French squadron had taken refuge. The giant *Foudroyant* (eighty-four) which had carried Galissonière to triumph over Byng, was fought to a standstill by Byng's old flag captain in the *Monmouth* (sixty-four). The French were soon dismantling in Toulon and British commerce with Spain and Italy revived. In America the action contributed to the fall of Louisburg which opened up the prospect of conquering Canada the following year.

The imminent collapse of her world overseas drove France

in 1759 to make her greatest effort. Choiseul was Pitt's equal in
energy and vision, and he saw that delay was to Britain's advantage. He planned a direct invasion to be made possible by the
junction of the Mediterranean and Atlantic fleets at Brest. Pitt
coolly pushed on with the Canadian campaign, but took the
precaution of strengthening the Mediterranean squadron and
appointing his toughest admiral to the command. Boscawen
soon had the south of France astir, but in June he was compelled
to withdraw to Gibraltar to revictual and repair, substituting
an open for the close blockade. Luck was with him, for de la
Clue, seeing his chance, came out with a dozen heavies and
three frigates in an attempt to steal along the Barbary coast and
run swiftly through the Gut by night. It was after dark on
17 August when an English frigate brought the news into
Gibraltar. Boscawen and his chief officers were dining with the
governor of San Roque. But on the flagship someone gave the
signal to unmoor. It was seen from San Roque and a few hours
later the great fleet of the line was standing out to sea in pursuit.
The reward came the next afternoon in the crushing victory of
Lagos Bay.

This success, followed closely by the destruction of the
Brest fleet at Quiberon, ended any remaining chance of a French
victory outside Europe. At the same time France's economy was
so exposed to the pressure of sea power that it seemed improbable
she would be much longer in a position to negotiate a satisfactory peace. The accession of Don Carlos late in the year as
Charles III of Spain was therefore especially welcome to
Choiseul. There is no denying that the Anglophil policies of
Ferdinand had made Britain's triumphs easier and altered the
balance of power to Spain's disadvantage. The news of Quebec,
Charles declared, froze his heart. He welcomed Choiseul's
approaches, though he was too discreet to consider intervening
before the time was ripe.

Pitt had done all in his power to conciliate Spain, for the
danger of a Bourbon reunion was an obsession with him. But
the moment he saw his gestures were unavailing he took bold
steps to meet the new situation. His favourite admiral, Saunders,
fresh from the St. Lawrence, was given the Mediterranean
command and ordered, while closely blockading the south of

France, to keep a wary eye on the Spanish ports. Pitt refused to be diverted by the peace offensive launched by George III on his accession in October 1760. His Belleîle expedition, undertaken in part to win a security for the restoration of Minorca, coincided with Choiseul's offer of a separate peace. When Belleîle fell in June 1761 his tone hardened. When in July Choiseul suggested that Spain be invited to guarantee the projected treaty, he read between the lines the signature of another Bourbon agreement, and proposed forthwith to strike at the treasure fleet to sever this last artery of Bourbon credit.

As is well known Pitt's colleagues rejected his proposals and the great minister resigned. But events showed him to have been right. A new Family Compact envisaged joint pressure on Portugal, the return of Minorca to Spain, and the beginning of formal hostilities at a convenient moment *after* the arrival of the *flota*. With Spain at last committed, Choiseul determined to use the new strategic possibilities to try invasion again. By invading Portugal, besieging Gibraltar and concentrating a combined armament at Ferrol, he hoped to divert the British fleet from the Channel and lay the south coast bare. However, Pitt's general strategy had been retained. Saunders was reinforced and from December 1761 onwards lay before Cadiz, while his frigates harried enemy shipping and watched Toulon. His skill and that of Hawke in handling their blockading squadrons defeated Choiseul's schemes. Indeed, the entry of Spain into the war was soon offset by the loss of Martinique and Cuba and of many rich prizes.

The Peace of Paris (1763) was not such as Pitt would have made. Its very virtues told against it. By not being severe enough it left France the means of recovery. By being still too severe it nourished a spirit of revenge. To the Mediterranean it scarcely applied. Minorca was returned to Britain in exchange for Belleîle. For France to have kept the island would have fatally prejudiced the Bourbon compact. Gibraltar was not mentioned. Its retention by Britain seemed to Choiseul the surest pledge of Franco-Bourbon solidarity, and he was by no means persuaded of its naval value. In Italy there was no change. The course of the war had, however, set back France's bid for commercial dominion of the Mediterranean. If British trade had been depressed in the early years of the war, before it ended French trade had been practically extinguished. Britain's total losses were heavier, but that was because she had so many more ships at sea.

Great as were Britain's gains from the Seven Years War, they were largely transitory. The policy of aggrandizement at the periphery ignored the need for a sound policy at the centre, that is to say, in Europe. Neither in America nor in the Mediterranean did the Bourbons accept their setback in any spirit of resignation. Spurred on by Choiseul France took over the positions in Europe that Britain was relinquishing. A first step was the acquisition of Corsica. Using her growing influence over the republic of Genoa, she bought the island outright in 1768 and completed the conquest the next year in time for Napoleon Bonaparte to be born a French citizen. Corsica not only guarded Toulon, whose dockyards it supplied with timber, but covered much of the Italian world, including Leghorn. The contrast between the passivity of British ministers on this occasion and their vigour in rebuffing Spain a year or two later over the Falkland Islands is the measure of the swing of mercantile interest away from the Mediterranean.

The Italian peninsula settled down into a Bourbon preserve. A network of alliances linked Austria with Tuscany, Spain Parma, Naples, Sardinia and France, and the whole was drawn together in 1770 by the marriage of the Dauphin with Marie Antoinette. Malta, likewise, came under French influence and its dockyards supplemented those of Toulon. In North Africa the Marseilles merchants developed their concessions at Bona and La Calle, and in the Eastern Mediterranean their growing competition was reflected in the declining fortunes of the Levant Company.

In face of this French pressure Britain gradually withdrew until her trade was more than ever centred on the still flourishing free port of Leghorn. Elsewhere it was dwindling. Gibraltar's trade was down, Minorca's insignificant. From Naples and Sicily came disappointing reports, though British cottons were beginning to be known. The currant trade was shifting from Zante to the Morea. Even in the Mediterranean Britain was feeling the effect of economic nationalism, adding its weight to the movement towards freer markets overseas.

If Britain's trade was thus reduced, her power was least affected among the Barbary States, where the possession of Gibraltar and Minorca gave her an advantage in dealing with the corsair chieftains. These were always impressed by the visible armaments, and appreciated the benefit of the long-term contracts for meat and provisions. The perpetual changes of ruler, each requiring independent recognition and expensive presents, gave much scope for international jockeying. But Britain was too well versed in the technique of Barbary negotiation to be easily outdone. Indeed, if anything could be more revolting than the cruelties practised by the corsairs, it was the corruption of Christian morals which all dealings with them seemed to entail.

This, broadly, was the state of the Mediterranean, when news of the rout at Lexington in April 1775 announced the outbreak of the American Revolution and showed Britain's day of reckoning to be near. Thanks to the efforts of Choiseul and Grimaldi the navies of France and Spain were stronger than ever before. They contrasted ominously with that of George III's England, so recently victorious, but now eaten through with corruption in timbers and management, only the men still sound. Nevertheless, both countries began cautiously, France waiting till after Saratoga before intervening, Spain till the summer of 1779. By this time Portugal and Morocco had been edged out of the British orbit, it being Charles III's intention to recover Gibraltar now whatever the cost. To Britain, on the other hand, the Mediterranean was again outside the main stream of war, which rapidly took the form of a struggle for survival. The two fortresses were in good condition, thanks to their governors, but it had not been possible to reinforce the small Mediterranean squadron.

The gates of Gibraltar were closed on 21 June 1779 and the Great Siege began. The garrison had only four months supplies, and 14,000 Spaniards settled down to starve it into surrender. Almost at once, therefore, a relief had somehow to be got in. With unusual resolution the Government spared a large part of the Home Fleet, its only resource, to save the fortress. On 29 December Rodney set out to escort the Gibraltar relief and with it the West India trade. Where the French and Spanish seemed paralysed by the winter storms Rodney was inspired. Off Finisterre he took a score of Spanish victuallers. Outside Gibraltar itself on 16 January he seized the Spanish admiral and seven of his blockading squadron. When the great fleet at last got in the triumph was intoxicating, the relief sufficient to support the defence for a further year.

It was a monotonous and grim year, with scurvy barely held in check. By the time it ended Britain herself, having gone to war with Holland and antagonized all the northern neutrals, was fighting alone against the greatest combination of sea power she had ever had to face. Yet the grand fleet had once more to be diverted. In April 1781 Admiral Darby reached the bay with 28 of the line and 100 storeships, having run the gauntlet of superior fleets in Brest and Cadiz. It was a magnificent achievement but a costly one. Preoccupied with his victuallers, he let de Grasse and Suffren out of Brest with fleets that turned the scales in America and India. But by now Gibraltar embodied the pride of a nation at bay and could not be sacrificed.

Bitterly disappointed, Spain turned to make sure of Minorca. Sailing from Cadiz the Duke de Crillon landed at Ciudadella on 19 August 1781 and closed in on the harbour of Mahon from either side. After a vain attempt to bribe General Murray he sat down patiently to starve him out. Murray was still feeling confident when, in December, a pernicious scurvy made its appearance and the garrison began to waste away. On 5 February 1782 he had to capitulate. Out of 2,700 men only 600 marched out, but all except 200 of the casualties had been due to disease. Afterwards, where Blakeney had been made a peer, Murray was found guilty by court-martial. One of Wolfe's ablest brigadiers and an enlightened administrator, he deserved better of his country.

Yorktown having already fallen (October 1781), peace was only a matter of time when Spain determined to eliminate at least one formidable ground of controversy by a final grand assault upon Gibraltar. So far, little impression had been made on its defences, although most of the town had been destroyed. The arrival of Crillon in June 1782 with 40,000 men quickened every pulse. To hasten proceedings General Boyd suggested the application of some red-hot shot to the strongest enemy batteries. They blew up, a very heartening sign. After that the bombardment was ceaseless day and night, by sea and land. On 12 September the Combined Fleets sailed into the Bay with ten powerful floating batteries specially designed by the French inventor, d'Arçon, to be virtually unsinkable. While the Isthmus guns kept up their bombardment, at dawn on the 13th the assault was joined from the sea. All that day and the next night the Peninsula shook with the thunder of 400 guns. The Rock, the Bay and the Isthmus were hidden in the smoke and flames. General Elliot, who commanded, grew very anxious when, after six hours, his fire had still made no mark on the floating batteries. The red-hot balls were bouncing off. Then weight and heat began to tell. A lucky shot fired the flag battery and the resulting confusion turned the scale. At midnight d'Arçon ordered the remaining batteries to be blown up and by morning the battle was over.

Although intermittent fire was maintained for five more months all danger of defeat by direct assault had vanished. But the garrison was again nearing the end of its resources. Could a third relief be got in? All through the summer Lord Howe had been eluding superior enemy fleets in home waters, skilfully escorting essential convoys out and in. Dare he now challenge the enemy concentration in the Straits? On 11 September he left Spithead with a convoy of 130, 30 of them for Gibraltar, and an escort of 34 ships of the line. It took him a month to reach the Gut. A week more and he had manœuvred the convoy into the mole in the teeth of heavy weather and the entire enemy fleet. A momentary halt outside the Straits for the enemy to come up if he chose, and the great admiral sped back to England, the fortress saved.

By the Peace of Versailles signed on 20 January 1783 Minorca was ceded to Spain after nearly seventy years of foreign occupation. But the Rock remained British. It had caught the imagination of the British people. In an epic contest Britain had, on her own, taken the measure of the united Bourbon powers. Had it not been for the King's obsession with the Colonial conflict, she would undoubtedly have triumphed again. The war had been fought primarily on the seas though the Mediterranean had figured little in its strategy. Minorca had been left to its fate, being clearly inessential to the prosecution of a war outside Europe. But Gibraltar, though similarly outside the scope of general strategy, had in fact filled a remarkable diversionary role. Spain's absorption in its reconquest deflected not only her own resources but those of France as well. Indeed, it was largely this pull of Cadiz upon Brest that permitted British fleets to move freely in home waters. The one disturbing question was whether it had not been Britain's concern for Gibraltar in 1781 that allowed the Brest fleet out and led to the disaster of Yorktown.

CHAPTER IV

GIBRALTAR AND MINORCA,
1713-83

THE price of power in the Mediterranean, Britain found, was responsibility for the naval bases acquired there. She was obliged to devise forms of government, new in her colonial experience, which would at once satisfy the needs of war and trade and at the same time remain consistent with the conditions of cession. For by Articles Ten and Eleven of the Treaty of Utrecht Britain was required to exclude Moors and Jews from both Gibraltar and Minorca, guarantee the Roman Catholic religion there, and, in the case of Gibraltar, prohibit smuggling. Such limitations were reasonable from the Spanish point of view but might go far to nullify many of the advantages Britain hoped to reap. It will be convenient to consider the case of Minorca first.

Minorca is the second in size and most easterly of the Balearic Islands, 258 square miles in area, 30 miles long, and lies 20 miles north-east of Majorca. Its generally bleak and sterile appearance is accentuated by the tall, stone fences which afford crops and animals their chief protection from the perpetual winds. In the eighteenth century the mass of the people were swarthy, undernourished peasants and labourers, so inured to poverty as hardly to be enticed by economic incentives. Contributing a third of their earnings in taxes and dues, they were so wedded to custom that, to English amazement, they rejected the proffered "English Constitution" in favour of the "tyranny" they knew. Of all their qualities the most pleasing were their cleanliness, their carefree delight in the *fiesta*, and the vivacity of the womenfolk. Such middle-class as existed did so by courtesy of inherited status, being self-conscious but penniless. Education was confined to the convents.

Of the towns the capital, Ciudadella, seemed stagnant, the haunt of a parasitical nobility and clergy whose form of culture the northern mind could not grasp. Port Mahon alone seemed to hold out any promise. With its long reach of deep and sheltered harbour, wide enough for manœuvring the largest of vessels, it might be made a "magazine" of Mediterranean trade as well as a first-class naval base. The remaining towns were merely collections of hovels.

All observers agreed that the island could have no future until the ecclesiastical estates were broken up, the church's exemption from taxation removed, and the paralysing system of entail abolished. No one realized how attached the Minorquins were to their ancient ways, how jealous of their rights and privileges. There were only about 16,000 of them in 1713, and of these some 300 were clergy, mainly friars. It was Britain's first experience of governing a civilized but alien community which looked down on British values.

Because of a promise made, on instructions, by the Duke of Argyle in December 1712 Britain was bound in her own law to preserve the Minorquins in their civil rights, in addition to the religious ones protected by the Treaty. This meant that the new administration took over entire a maze of competing courts and authorities whose processes it did not understand. The most important of these, in many ways, were the local bodies known as Universities.

There were four Universities, one for each district. They were composed of Jurats and councillors chosen annually by lot from a list prepared by each University and forwarded to the Governor for revision. The result was a kind of functional representation of the different estates of nobles, citizens, merchants, artisans and peasants. Through these bodies the people controlled the supply of necessaries, fixed prices, levied certain taxes and had a say in the general government. It was in them that the Minorquins felt their liberties resided. They gave an impression of representative self-government, a principle to which the Minorquins believed themselves deeply attached.

Hitherto, British experience had been practically confined to North America and the West Indies where the colonists had taken with them British laws and institutions and insisted on their rights as these were understood by eighteenth-century Englishmen. In their constitutional theory the colonies were microcosms of England herself. Their governors, nominated councils and elected assemblies were replicas in miniature of King, Lords and Commons. By the Crown and ministers on the other hand colonial institutions were regarded more as local bodies, levying taxes in the form of rates and legislating by by-law. They were looked upon as subject, therefore, to the overriding executive power of the Crown.

The obvious parallel to the new Mediterranean dependencies was the old one of Tangier, and there the theory just outlined had been put into practice. Minorca, with its quasi-representative institutions, fitted surprisingly well into this theory and might be expected to conform readily provided local sentiment were respected. The collapse of the Old Colonial System in Minorca was to be due, indeed, less to constitutional or fiscal grievances than to racial and religious bigotry.

In the first period of the British occupation of Minorca one man stood out as pioneer of an enlightened imperial tradition. This was Colonel Richard Kane who came to the island in 1713 as Lieutenant-Governor to the absentee Earl of Portmore and soon found himself in trouble with both clergy and Jurats. In 1718 the Privy Council investigated the island's affairs and on its advice Kane, in 1721, issued his Code of Seventeen Articles, designed to effect a religious settlement. Minorca was brought within the pale of the Anglican establishment by cutting off Roman Catholics there from dependence on Spain or Rome and limiting ecclesiastical offices to natives of the island who took the oath of allegiance. The dues owed to the Bishop of Majorca were paid into the Minorquin treasury. But a certain connection with the Bishop had to be kept up in order to ordain the priesthood and so "preserve" the Church in accordance with Article Eleven.

Kane did much for the island. He carried out overdue legal reforms, relieved the perennial indebtedness of the Universities, shifted the seat of government from the clerical headquarters at Ciudadella to Mahon where the fleet lay, and built the great road across the island still named after him. His concern for the well-being of the people, the diminution of crime and the economic improvement under his rule, above all, his "gentleness", have led Minorquins to remember him with affection.

But under the less responsible rule of Kane's successors petty vexations were sufficient to cause bad feeling and bring into existence an anti-British party. One governor was brought to trial in England for "private oppression" and "embezzling public money". A spark was enough in 1749 to set the island ablaze with religious fury. Some officers assisted three nuns to escape from their convent and afterwards sought permission to marry them in the Protestant faith. Priests and parents shook with the outrage. For once in his life the Duke of Newcastle sent back an immediate answer to the Governor's appeal for directions. General Blakeney dealt with the question so judiciously, however, that within a few months all anger was spent and the wives settled down almost alongside their former convent.

In 1731 and again in 1752 the home government went into the matter of reforming the constitution. In the latter year General Blakeney, already in trouble with the Church and the Universities, was sent regulations which increased the responsibilities of the Jurats and limited the Governor's powers in finance and administration. An attempt was made at the same time to reduce the burden of requisitions on the civil population. It was a praiseworthy endeavour to make the best of the island's existing institutions and was well received by the Minorquins.

However, on Blakeney's complaint that the Jurats were intoxicated with their new powers and cornering the meat which the army needed, further Regulations were sent out in August 1753. Ostensibly these cleared up some ambiguities, but in reality they gave the Governor more power over the Jurats and tightened up the execution of Kane's Articles even to the extent of prohibiting Minorquins from going abroad for their education. One overdue reform was, indeed, adopted. The civil power was separated from the military and appeals to the King permitted, so filling in a gap which had held up some cases for forty years.

In their frustration, the Minorquins declared the latest Regulations a breach of both the Promise and the Treaty, and claimed, like other British colonies, a permanent agent in London to protect their interests. The agitation resulted in their

E

setting up an alternative body of Jurats, who began the unofficial direction of affairs. Firm measures had to be taken to restore the Governor's authority. By 1755 the situation was sufficiently in hand again for Blakeney, following a Gibraltar precedent, to permit a pastoral visit from the Bishop of Majorca, thereby, however, admitting his jurisdiction.

By Article Twelve of the Peace of Paris (1763) Minorca was restored to Britain on the same terms as before, and the first Lieutenant-Governor, Johnston, being temperamentally unsuited for his task, managed less well than Blakeney. The appointment of General James Murray in 1774, however, was symptomatic of a change of attitude. It was this pugnacious Scot who had so enraged the English community in Quebec by his open sympathy with the French Canadians.

Murray went about his task characteristically by having his salary put on a fixed basis, free from dependence on fees and perquisites, even if it meant some personal loss. Studying the Constitution, he told the Jurats he intended to follow it strictly, but promised to lay before the King any changes they thought desirable. A legal establishment five hundred years old, he reported home, needed modifying to meet the needs of an island now decidedly prosperous. He considered the people moral, respectful and well disposed; but the financial chaos of the Universities would never be removed until power had been transferred from the "indigent and ignorant" to the "opulent and well-informed", and their share in the upkeep of the troops set at a fixed amount. It was a premonition of the British Imperial version of benevolent despotism.

The outbreak of war with the American Colonies prevented much action being taken along these lines. Murray was distressed to find his efforts at conciliation largely unappreciated. It was, perhaps, the just commentary on the incapacity of the old colonial technique to meet the case of a people like the Minorquins, of different race and religion, that notwithstanding the improvement in general welfare, the fall of the British administration in the very act of transforming itself was accompanied by widespread disaffection. Only four Minorquins took part in the defence of 1781-2.

*   *   *   *   *

Gibraltar, unlike Minorca, contained no native community, so no question arose of maintaining any existing constitution. A purely military government might have seemed the only and obvious solution. Yet at the very outset Britain showed herself to be of two minds over Gibraltar. In February 1706 it was declared a free port; and in 1720, in answer to merchants' petitions, a Charter was conceded. This set up a Court Merchant composed of the military judge-advocate and two merchants with powers of summary jurisdiction over civil pleas. It was foundation enough for further pretensions.

This early provision for trade gives a clue to the otherwise bewildering attitude of Britain towards the fortress during the next century and a half. Ministers hesitated whether to regard Gibraltar more as fortress or as *entrepôt*. The interests represented on the Rock were those they themselves stood for at home. If theirs was the responsibility for national security, nevertheless to all alike military rule was inherently suspect. Consequently, the persistence of the "garrison" type of government at Gibraltar was chiefly due to its being in operation there already, and to the Government being too undecided to risk a deliberate change. The diplomatic effects of this irresolution have already been noticed.

Gibraltar also differed from Minorca in having no natural resources. Everything had to be brought in either from England or from neighbouring states like Spain or Barbary. This made the treaty restrictions so much the more onerous. Religion was less of a stumbling block than in Minorca, but the prohibition both of Jews and Moors and of smuggling would have been economically disastrous. The Jews, with their valuable connections with Barbary and Italy, gradually filtered in to become the backbone of the *entrepôt* trade. Observance of the rules against the Moors would have run contrary to existing treaties with them and prejudiced essential North African supplies. To put an end to smuggling, finally, would have destroyed the merchants' *raison d'être* and greatly reduced the value of the Rock.

The number of substantial British merchant houses remained stationary at about a dozen, but the population grew rapidly as the *entrepôt* attracted the most polyglot and unsavoury

characters from all parts of the Mediterranean. The governors
military men chosen for quite other reasons than their fitness fo
so delicate an office, had the greatest difficulty enforcing thei
authority, much less the rules against smuggling, and wer
always at loggerheads with the inhabitants.

The Civil Court had no power to try crimes. Had th
Governor, then, a prerogative authority to deal with criminal
by proclamation and expulsion? If so, did any writ run on th
neutral ground or in the harbour beyond reach of the guns? If
for the security of the garrison, a check had to be kept on th
consumption of strong drink, did the Governor have authorit
in a free port to enforce his orders against the scores of vendors
Were members of the garrison liable to be whisked away from
essential military duties to serve sentence for debt? In ever
instance where the law officers in England were consulted the
gave their opinion against "arbitrary rule".

Some remedy had to be attempted. First the Tangie
precedent was thought of, and in 1729 a draft Charter of Incor
poration was prepared, constituting mayor, aldermen and
councillors. This might have enabled Gibraltar to develop
some form of civic life. But the "British colony" was alarmed
at the prospect of being swamped by foreigners and in 1738 th
idea was dropped on the Governor's representation that th
number of loyal Protestant British subjects was too small fo
a corporation to be chosen from them. Ministers were reminded
moreover, that whatever its commercial status, at critica
moments Gibraltar would again become a "meer Garrison'
fighting for its life.

In May 1740 a more modest reform was tried, a new judicia
establishment which would have given the Governor th
reserve powers he needed. Unfortunately, although the judge
was appointed and paid neither he nor the Charter ever arrived
in the colony. Confusion mounted because the Charter was
acted upon in certain respects just as if it had been regularl
promulgated.

The next step was the mission of General Humphrey Bland
in 1749. In less than two years Bland made a thorough survey o
every branch of Gibraltar's affairs and issued a series o
Ordinances which, as "General Bland's Regulations", governed

he life of the colony for the next sixty years. He tried to reduce
he danger to security by gradually transferring landed property
nto Protestant hands and laying down strict rules for the
ntroduction and sale of spirits; to improve the town's internal
conomy by levying a scavenger's rate and controlling prices
nd weights and measures; to deal at once firmly and honour-
bly with the Moors; and, above all, to regain Spanish goodwill
y suppressing smuggling and observing the health laws.

In all these ways Bland did achieve a temporary improvement, perhaps mainly because he was personally disinterested
n the fees and perquisites which the Gibraltar command
notoriously afforded. But after he left, no Regulations could
prevent the old system gradually creeping back again. He was
east happy, moreover, in his judicial recommendations. The
Charter issued on his advice in 1752 was a compromise affair.
Ignoring the 1740 Charter, it merely extended the civil jurisdic-
ion of the existing Court Merchant and set up in addition three
ustices of the peace (Governor, judge-advocate and a merchant)
o hear criminal causes. This left most of the legal problems
unsolved and loaded the judge-advocate with additional and
often contradictory duties.

Thus administered, and with a population which in 1725
already numbered 1,100, of whom only 100 were British,
Gibraltar grew into a kind of Mediterranean shanty town. It
was dingy, insanitary, and ridden with disease and vice. Visitors
were appalled by its motley denizens: "Jews, Genoese,
Spaniards, Portuguese, Irish Papists, Scotch pedlars and
English bankrupts!... the riff-raff of various nations and religions
ready to commit any fraud in their power"—so General Bland
described them. Under bombardment shops and private
residences suffered most, so little care was taken in building or
planning. The destruction of the Great Siege would have been a
blessing had not the whole disorderly process been allowed to
begin again.

Commercially, the advantage lay with Gibraltar. Although
many Minorquins profited from the needs of the garrison and
the expenditure on public works and some secured government
employment, the island remained economically backward. The

chief benefit was drawn by its shipping, which had long carried coral, fish and corn. Protected by the British Mediterranean passes, the small craft ranged the coasts of the Western Mediterranean and engrossed more than their share of the carrying trade, especially in corn and beef for the garrison. In war time moreover, equipped (or not) with British letters of marque Minorquin privateers bit into the French North African trade across the routes of which the island lay. But this was all on a small scale, and contemporary representations of the island' value to British commerce are misleading.

To Gibraltar, on the contrary, the British occupation spelt unexampled prosperity. The Rock very soon became a general *entrepôt* from which the monopolies of Old and New Spain were breached and fresh cargoes loaded for the Mediterranean carrying trade. By 1736 exports to Gibraltar and the Straits reached a peak of £1,000,000, a figure exceeded by only four other trades. But the feature that most appealed to contemporary economists was the fact that these sales were paid for in hard cash and so contributed largely to Britain's favourable balance of trade. Between 1736 and 1763 there was a slight decline and after that the fall was steep. In all, nevertheless, it was an extraordinary consumption for a fortress!

This great trade consisted chiefly of British woollens and ironware for the Spanish home and colonial market, usually disposed of via Cadiz, together with re-exported West Indian produce like tobacco and sugar for smuggling into Andalusia. The contraband was carried on, conveniently, by the Spanish themselves. In their tiny boats they were adept at evading the army of corrupt Customs officials stationed along the coast.

As a free port, moreover, where ships of all countries could deposit and exchange their cargoes, Gibraltar was so well situated as to rival even Leghorn. The Barbary States, Morocco in particular, supplied the garrison with the meat, fresh vegetables and fruit essential to its health. In the same small boats came typical North African produce, wax and dates, Moroccan leather, ivory and ostrich feathers, all for re-export to Spain, France or Italy in return for their wines, oils and silks. Mules from Morocco were sold to the West Indian plantations in exchange for rum and coffee. Salt fish from Newfound-

and was a regular article of trade to meet the religious requirements of the Latin countries, the ships that carried it completing
a triangular traffic by loading Mediterranean cargoes for London
and Bristol.

During the first half of the century Gibraltar also contributed
largely to Britain's pre-eminence in the Mediterranean carrying
trade by providing ships laden for the Peninsula further profitable port-to-port cargoes, until they could turn back with the
regular import from Smyrna, Zante or Leghorn. Lumber
ships from New England used the same technique. The proceeds
were taken mainly in bullion, whether for shipment home or
for use up the Mediterranean to reduce the drain on specie to
Italy and Turkey. There grew up in this way a reserve of buying
power upon which the Government could draw to pay and
provision the naval and military services in those seas.

Minorca, on the other hand, was the more highly valued as
an instrument of war. For enabling the fleet to fulfil its primary
purpose of acting against Toulon, it was much more favourably
placed. Its greatest distinction, however, was in its harbour of
Port Mahon, consisting of a land-locked bay three and a half
miles long by a third of a mile wide, deep and almost tideless and
with a narrow, protected entrance. Mahon, the city, lay snugly
on the innermost shore, together with the Navy's wharves,
storehouses, repair yards and powder magazine. Three miles
down, guarding the mouth, sat the Castle of St. Philip's, a
triumph of fortress building and, when properly garrisoned,
secure against assault.

As a naval harbour, Port Mahon was thus superb, especially
for a fleet on the offensive. But in British hands it had one fatal
weakness. It could not be used once an enemy had landed sufficient forces in the island to pen up the garrison in St. Philip's. In
that event the entire anchorage and line of naval yards and
buildings was left unguarded. Such a hostile enterprise was not,
moreover, very difficult, and the passage from Majorca could
be accomplished by small boats in a night. Experience showed
also that when the main theatres of war were elsewhere than the
south of France or Spain the mere effort to protect the island
strained the Navy's resources. Naval protection could never be

withdrawn from Minorca for even a short time without risk to the whole naval establishment. If that fell, it was small consolation to the Fleet that St. Philip's was still holding out.

Gibraltar suffered from none of these defects. In a military sense the Rock was impregnable. The peninsula on which Gibraltar stands runs about three and a half miles due south. The first mile is a low isthmus of sand upon which the sheer face of the rock, rising to a thousand feet, suddenly abuts. The only way round was to the west, and that past a morass and then by a narrow avenue readily commanded by the fortress's guns. On the east, the Mediterranean side, the mountain face was quite inaccessible.

Accordingly, great military works were constructed to guard the north-west approach and to command the sands and the Spanish lines across them. Here there arose a question of territorial jurisdiction. The British claim was that in peace time Gibraltar should be understood to have the privilege of a fortress, that is to say, notwithstanding Article Ten, jurisdiction as far as the point-blank range of her guns, or about 500 yards. From the outset British sentries, ignoring Spanish protests, occupied the Devil's Tower beyond the north-east corner. Their persistence in this slowly produced the idea of a Neutral Ground.

Once an enemy should obtain local command at sea, the waterfront looking across the bay to Algeçiras was seen to be the most likely place of attack. Success there would lead directly on to the town and disrupt the shipping at the Old and New Moles. The Old Mole, actually within gunshot of the Isthmus, was reserved for commerce, though the larger merchantmen could not berth there. The New Mole, a mile or more south beyond the town, was the naval headquarters. To protect these, especially the latter, was therefore a principal object of engineering skill. Just in time for the Great Siege Sir Robert Boyd, who as Lieutenant-Governor and then Governor, watched over the defences for nearly thirty years, got the stout King's Bastion at last constructed, with great effect.

Landings from the southward over the shoals at Europa Point, where the rock falls in terraces down to fifty-foot cliffs at the water's edge, though always feared, were never attempted.

The currents were fierce and the loss of men and landing craft was evidently thought too great a risk. Again it was Boyd who gave extra security by his works at Windmill Hill.

Gibraltar's defects were not on the military but on the naval side, and partly due to neglect. In the small naval yard only superstructures could be repaired as the hulls of vessels could not be raised. The naval hospital had to be shared with the garrison. The victualling yard was efficiently run, but facilities for watering were not so good as those at Tetuan on the African coast, which was more generally used. As a harbour the Bay was not very satisfactory, being swept by Atlantic gales which drove craft aground. Though the passage of an enemy fleet could be observed in most weathers, it was hardly possible to intercept if, as was to be expected, it had a favourable wind. Indeed, far from naval squadrons being habitually stationed at Gibraltar, as is sometimes supposed, it was unusual to find so much as a frigate in the roadstead for purposes of police or the transmission of news.

Thus Gibraltar was superior to Minorca militarily and economically, but inferior to it as an offensive naval weapon. Had it not been for the exceptional experience of the Seven Years War and the War of American Independence in which the Mediterranean was less important in general strategy, Britain would probably have preferred to give up Gibraltar rather than Minorca. Indeed, when occasion again arose to act offensively up the Mediterranean, the island had once more to be secured until a still better base had been acquired.

CHAPTER V

THE GREAT WAR WITH FRANCE, 1783-1815

(a) 1783-1802

THE loss of the American Colonies coincided with the impact of the Industrial Revolution and helped produce a revolution also in imperial policy. Exulting in her industrial expansion and confident of her Navy, Britain gradually swung over from her mercantilist past to embrace the Free Trade ideal. In this progress of more than half a century, colonies of the former settlement type lost their importance and interest focused on the east and the tropics, where great profits could be made from trade without, it was hoped, the old embarrassing political complications. If colonies there must be, it was felt, they should not again be colonies of white settlement unless perhaps for strategic reasons.

The change of attitude was reflected in the Cabinet of the younger Pitt where Henry Dundas held a commanding position. Dundas was variously responsible for Indian affairs, colonies and war and never relaxed his care for the India routes, whether that *via* the Cape or the embryo one through Egypt in which the French grew increasingly interested.

If, between 1784 and 1786, ministers listened to proposals for returning Gibraltar in exchange for an Anglo-Spanish *entente*, that was because France was then on the verge of entering Holland and so securing not only the Dutch fleet and the best invasion ports, but control of the Cape route as well. For similar reasons Pitt was less disturbed by the early phases of the French Revolution than by the affair of the China merchants at Nootka Sound on the west coast of Canada. The moment Spain gave way on that matter he ventured his famous prediction of fifteen years of peace (17 February 1792).

So far out was Pitt in his reckoning, however, that within a year all Europe was under arms to restrain the Revolutionaries and he himself was organizing the first of his great coalitions. The eastern monarchies were chiefly interested in partitioning Poland, but, the Bourbon family union having collapsed, Britain found herself fighting on much the same lines as in the early days of Anne. Once again it became important to secure a base up the Mediterranean from which to support her allies and act against Toulon. Though financial considerations made a West Indian expedition desirable, nevertheless the way was open for a Mediterranean offensive, as it had not been in 1756 or 1778. Sardinia had lost Nice and Savoy. Austria required naval support to shield her Italian interests, and Naples, already attacked by a squadron from Toulon, refused to move without British assistance. Spain's anxiety to protect Catalonia soothed the rancour aroused by the Nootka controversy and promised a return to the conditions of Marlborough's war.

Subsidy treaties being prepared with each of these states, late in June 1793 a fleet under Lord Hood pushed through the Straits to take up the blockade of Toulon and assist the Sardinians and Austrians along the Riviera. Then, quite unexpectedly, on 29 August, the great base was delivered into his keeping by Royalists who had gained command of the town. It was a stroke such as might have fittingly concluded a hard-fought campaign, and Hood called in Spaniards, Neapolitans and Piedmontese to help him garrison the fifteen-mile perimeter. At home, ministers hastened to divert resources already pledged elsewhere, and soon contrived such a game of shuttlecock (acting on reports of the situation always three weeks out of date) that much of Britain's military contribution hardly left the high seas during the next half year.

If the Allies had felt any sense of urgency about the outcome of the war, Toulon might possibly have been held. Instead it became merely a source of discord. Where co-operation would in any case have been difficult Hood's rough tactlessness was provocative. Spain became alarmed at this "second Gibraltar" and Linzee's expedition to Corsica in support of the insurgent Paolists, though it turned out unsuccessfully, confirmed her fears. Nor could the Civil Commissioner, Gilbert Elliot, persuade the old officer to moderate his strident tone towards the small states of Genoa and Tuscany, perilously stranded between France and Austria by land and Britain by sea.

In spite of famine caused by the allied blockade of their coast, the French armies steadily closed in on the port until in mid-December it had to be evacuated. Most of the French warships and part of the arsenal being hurriedly burnt by Sir Sidney Smith, on the 19th the two fleets withdrew and separated, taking with them 7,500 refugees. It was now imperative to secure another base. So once again Hood sent to Paoli with a view to occupying Corsica.

During 1794 the Mediterranean scene was dominated by this Corsican adventure. Britain took advantage of the island's nationalist aspirations to unite it to the Crown, hoping to turn it into a superior Minorca. Sir Gilbert Elliot's powers were extended until he was exercising a kind of pro-consular authority, trying to harness the Italian states into a system of common defence and, as Viceroy of Corsica, forwarding British interests in the central Mediterranean. The course of Anglo-Corsican relations is dealt with in the following chapter. Here need be noted only the long delays imposed by the sturdy resistance of the Republicans in their three coastal strongholds and sustained by the humiliating disagreements between Lord Hood and successive military commanders. Unhappy examples of combined operations, these sieges are chiefly remembered for the bravery and initiative of Colonel John Moore and Captain Horatio Nelson, both of them wounded at Calvi which did not surrender till 10 August.

In these circumstances neither Hood nor the military commander-in-chief, Charles Stuart, could undertake the offensive operations in the south of France which the Government had intended. While the French made ready to advance on Piedmont and Genoa Hood's activity was confined to the economic blockade. Elliot, returning despondently from a mission to Turin and Milan, recognized that there was little hope of getting even these two courts to co-operate, much less of uniting all Italy. Nevertheless, the disappointments elsewhere from Holland to the West Indies, made the small gains in the Mediterranean seem important. If the strength of Corsica could only be built up so as to give confidence to Britain's friends, the gathering waves of Republicanism might still be stemmed.

These hopes were not realized. The fall of Holland the next year (1795) broke up the northern front and renewed Pitt's earlier fears. Nervous for India Dundas sent an expedition to secure the Cape, but it would hardly have got past Brest had not French forces there been depleted to mount a new Mediterranean challenge. When, early in March, the French came out to recover Corsica, Admiral Hotham brought them to battle in the timorous engagement that provoked Nelson's historic comment. So reduced was his squadron, indeed, by two years' service far from a repair base that for him and for Corsica victory might have been as bad as defeat. Unfortunately this was no isolated incident. One French squadron escaped from Toulon and carried a Turkey convoy into Cadiz. Another was allowed to roam the Levant at leisure and return with all its prizes. Supported only by Nelson in *Agamemnon* the Allied land campaign excusably broke down, and in November the combined armies, beaten at Loano, fell back in confusion across the Maritime Alps leaving the coast route open.

When Bonaparte first took over the Italian command, in March 1796, this strategic situation had hardly altered. But the Peninsula was now permeated with the revolutionary virus. A single swift movement from Savona in April thrust the Allies back on their separate bases at Turin and Milan. By the middle of May Sardinia had made peace, Bonaparte himself was in Milan, and the Austrians had been swept back on Mantua and their famous Quadrilateral. In June, preparatory to forcing this last line, Bonaparte turned south to Tuscany and the Papal States. The Leghorn merchants fled to Corsica. Elliot looked on uneasily at the influx of spies and agitators and the gathering of Corsican exiles on the surrounding coasts. Even the iron spirit of Sir John Jervis, who now assumed the naval command, could hardly restore the situation if Corsica were lost and supplies cut off by Bonaparte's further advance.

Jervis's task was indeed a difficult one. Elliot's Corsican administration was already tottering. Naples was divided by rival factions. The growth of Spanish hostility threatened his communications with England. A big part of his fleet being taken up with supply and trade protection, all he could spare his Imperial ally was a small flotilla in the upper Adriatic. By the summer it was fairly clear that Corsica would fall, so Elliot seized Elba as an alternative base. Bonaparte, meanwhile, undistracted by his southern flirtation, dealt the Austrian armies relieving Mantua a series of staggering blows during August and September. Then he turned south again to fan Italian national aspirations by creating a republic in central Italy. On 4 August French ships were ominously escorted out to sea from Cadiz by the Spanish fleet.

However, the decision was taken not in the Mediterranean but in Whitehall. For Pitt and his colleagues the war had for some time been losing its ideological urgency. The France of the Directory was neither "democratic" nor regicide. Peace feelers had already been put out. That autumn, when a supreme combined effort might still have turned the scale, when Bonaparte was awaiting the last Austrian sweeps on Mantua, negotiations were resumed at Paris and orders sent to evacuate Corsica and withdraw the fleet to the shelter of the Tagus. Justification followed in November when the Spanish declared war. But the step did mean that Austria was left without support at a moment when she was testing Bonaparte to the limit in the marshes of Arcola (15 November 1796).

The withdrawal from the Mediterranean was, indeed, a grave step. It meant, in effect, that in a period of extreme national peril Britain preferred to carry on alone. Alarmed for the safety of Ireland and of Portugal ministers allowed Earl Spencer at the Admiralty to impose on them strategical principles adapted to the Navy's strained resources. By concentrating his strength Spencer hoped to hold the Channel and Atlantic with thirty sail off Brest, and in the south-west to reinforce Jervis to a like extent.

This was a defensive but still a bold strategy, and it more than achieved its purpose. Portugal was saved, an attempt on Ireland from Brest frustrated. In the middle of February 1797 the main Spanish fleet, leaving the Mediterranean to join the Brest fleet in a grand sweep of the Channel, was shattered off Cape St. Vincent by Jervis and Nelson with half its numbers.

Nelson, who had only the day before got back from a dare-devil run up the Mediterranean to evacuate the naval stores from Elba, became a national hero and received his recognition in the Order of the Bath. But the victory—"very essential to England at this hour"—was due to Spencer and Jervis.

The price of the nation's safety had to be paid in the Mediterranean. In April 1797 Austria bought a separate peace at Leoben, giving up Belgium and Lombardy in return for a share in the mainland of Venice. Bonaparte began his dream of the East. That October he obtained for France the Venetian fleet and—"more interesting to us than the whole of Italy"—the Ionian Islands. These included the superb naval harbour of Corfu, commanding the entrance to the Adriatic and abutting on Turkish Greece. French agents filtered into Malta where the national sentiments of the people and the preponderance of French knights in the Order of St. John opened up inviting channels of intrigue. While Britain was kept in alarm by an army at Boulogne, plans were concerted with Tipu Sahib to over-throw her power in India. At Toulon some great enterprise was seen to be preparing.

Austria, meanwhile, was discovering that treaties of peace put no stop to French aggrandizement, and began feeling her way towards renewed co-operation with Britain. Earl Spencer had no sooner completed his naval dispositions than pressure was put on him to lend assistance up the Mediterranean once again, to encourage Austria and protect Naples. In April 1798 he reluctantly instructed Jervis (now Earl St. Vincent) to send Nelson to sweep the Mediterranean. A mere defensive was clearly not enough.

St. Vincent had anticipated his Government and Nelson's small detachment only narrowly missed the departure of Bonaparte's massed armament from Toulon on 19 May. Unluckily, even when Troubridge joined him with ten sail of the line, Nelson still had no frigates and endured agonies of disappointment trying to sight Bruey's skilfully piloted fleet. One week only (June 12-19) Bonaparte paused in Malta, ignominiously surrendered by the Knights. A fortnight later he was in Egypt, a destination only Dundas had suspected.

Another month passed before Nelson came up at last with the
fleet that had so long eluded him and destroyed it utterly in
Aboukir Bay on 1 August 1798. Bonaparte and his splendid army
were cut off from France.

The triumph of the Nile made Britain once again a Mediter
ranean power. On news of it the Sultan moved his armies down
through Syria. The Tsar Paul, incensed by the wanton seizure
of Malta, accepted the grandmastership of the Order. The
combined navies of Russia and Turkey sailed through the
Bosphorus to occupy the Ionian Islands. The people of Malta
rose in revolt and shut the French in Valletta. In November
Naples, urged on by Nelson and the Hamiltons, recklessly
declared war on her own account, while Nelson blockaded the
Riviera and landed troops in Leghorn. Though two dismal
months passed before word of the battle reached England
ministers persisted in their forward policy. A small squadron
rounded the Cape for the Red Sea, and in the second week of
November Minorca fell to Duckworth and Stuart. Bluffing
brilliantly, they recovered the great naval base without the loss
of a man. Before the end of the year an alliance with Russia
laid the foundation of the Second Coalition.

After this Britain did not again relinquish her ascendancy in
the Mediterranean. The usual consequences followed. Beyond
Europe the tentacles of French power were cut or pushed in
Inside Europe Austria joined the Coalition and the Directory's
armies were thrust roughly back upon their frontiers until only
Allied dissension in the hour of victory saved the Republic. By
midsummer 1799 the army that had crushed the Neapolitans for
their temerity was itself locked up in Genoa. Back in England
Stuart, broken in health, was chafing at the opportunities being
lost through the absence of an English expeditionary force.

The Directory saw its danger and sent the Brest fleet to the
rescue of its ablest general. With twenty-five of the line and
ten frigates Admiral Bruix passed Lord Keith off Cadiz and on
5 May 1799 sped through the Straits. From the Rock the ailing
St. Vincent looked on helplessly as the whole Mediterranean
seemed in Bruix's grasp. St. Vincent's great fleet, dispersed on a
score of errands, frantically concentrated. Nelson, from Naples
stood off the little island of Marittimo where he could close the

Tunisian Channel and still be on hand to the west. Summoning Keith after him, St. Vincent raced for Mahon.

Fortunately for the Allies Bruix had no heart for the enterprise. Throwing a relief into Genoa he left Toulon for Cartagena into which, after Keith's departure, the Cadiz fleet had run. He would have been stopped had not Keith, over-anxious for Minorca, momentarily left his cruising station. Thence in July the great combined fleet passed the Straits a second time bound for Brest. Miserably managed though the incursion had been, it had let supplies into Valletta and broken the Cadiz blockade. To the Allies it was an omen that the sands of time were running out. That autumn the Russians withdrew from the war and Bonaparte, eluding Sidney Smith, landed safely in the south of France.

So far Britain's military contribution had been limited, in the Mediterranean, to the garrison at Minorca and a few weak battalions in the citadel of Messina. Early in 1800 Stuart's plans for an expeditionary force had been approved in principle by Cabinet, but before the Army got away, late in April, it had been shorn of half its numbers for an attempt on the Breton coast and its commander had resigned. The elderly Abercromby, who succeeded Stuart, was given to understand that his primary objective was Malta, but that Minorca, Naples and Portugal also needed protection and that Austria should be given all possible help. The movements of Abercromby's force were as cumbrous as his instructions and while Keith fretted at his inability to give the help by land which might have reduced Genoa and opened up the south of France, Bonaparte was preparing his thunderbolts. The expeditionary force was still no nearer than Minorca when the hard-won triumph of Marengo sealed the collapse of Italy.

The Second Coalition being now obviously doomed, there was little Britain could do but garner her harvest by sea. Plans were devised for attacking Brest and putting Spain out of the war by demolishing her arsenals at Ferrol and Cadiz. For this latter enterprise Abercromby's force was brought all the way back in October under escort of the main fleet, only to be saved from the ill-omened adventure by a timely storm. The one success was the surrender, at last, of the French garrison in Valletta. To

F

the chagrin of the Maltese, who had sustained the burden of the siege by land for two years, General Vaubois capitulated to the British military commander alone, on 5 September 1800.

Inconsequential as such policies may now seem, Bonaparte nevertheless saw in them the closing jaws of sea power. In August he anxiously proposed a maritime truce, under cover of which he hoped to relieve Malta and Egypt. He bore upon Spain to cede him Louisiana and, with all speed, to occupy Portugal. Malta, when it had already fallen, he offered as a bribe to the Tsar Paul, who was so far won over that in December 1800 he united the northern powers in a League of Armed Neutrals. Peace with Austria in February 1801 restored the 1797 arrangements in North Italy, while that with Naples the following month excluded British vessels from Neapolitan ports and admitted a French garrison into Otranto—an arrow pointing at Egypt.

The danger in the north was dispersed by Nelson's victory of Copenhagen and the accession of the friendly Tsar Alexander. That in the south was met by a timely reinforcement pushed into Lisbon and then, on Dundas's pressing initiative, by a series of concentric moves on Egypt. An inspired vision brought the resources of the New Empire into play against the common enemy. Popham from the Cape, Baird from Bombay came up the Red Sea. Keith supported Abercromby's army by way of Malta on to Egypt, where the old general laid down his life in the victory of Aboukir in March 1801.

The same month Addington succeeded Pitt as Prime Minister. The new Government immediately made an offer of peace on the basis of each side keeping what it had won. The nation was war-weary. France's inflated land power was at least confined to Europe and Englishmen felt reasonably secure with their great fleets and factories and open world markets.

A tussle accordingly ensued for bargaining counters. Portugal being compelled to exclude British shipping, Madeira was occupied in compensation for the Tagus. Ganteaume escaped from Brest in an endeavour to succour Egypt, but was driven into Toulon by the grim English pursuit. On 6 July three of his ships, under Linois, trying to join the Spanish in Cadiz, were forced beneath the guns of Algeçiras by a larger

orce under Admiral Saumarez. Saumarez attacked but, the
wind dropping, had to retire badly mauled into Gibraltar. The
naval yard set to with such a will, however, that five days later
the squadron was out again hard in pursuit of Linois and the
Spaniards who had reinforced him from Cadiz. In a rough
night's struggle off the coast west of Algeçiras Saumarez got
his revenge when two ships blew up and another was captured.

Nevertheless, Bonaparte was so far successful that British
ministers were bluffed into signing preliminaries of peace on
1 October 1801, the day before the news reached London that
Egypt had fallen. After that they were always at a disadvantage.
In return for his quitting the Egypt he had already lost, for his
guarantee of Britain's remaining allies, Turkey and Portugal,
and for a promise to withdraw from southern Italy, Britain
agreed to restore all except two of her oversea conquests. And
these two, great strategic and commercial assets though they
were, were at the expense not of France but of Holland and
Spain. It was overlooked that Britain had been given no say in
European reconstruction, intimately though it concerned her.
It was remembered too late that the promised restoration of the
Knights of St. John conflicted with Britain's own strategic
interests—for Bonaparte's *coup* could be repeated—and with
her admitted obligations to the Maltese people.

In these circumstances Britain appeared at the Conference
of Amiens as a supplicant for France's favours. Every concession
had its price. If Malta was not to be evacuated within the pre-
scribed month, then France would, after all, retain Otranto as
security. If no "third power" could be found ready to take the
island under its "guarantee and protection", then an all-power
guarantee would have to be substituted—a condition virtually
impossible to fulfil.

The extent of the failure of British statesmanship on this
occasion may be simply measured. In ten years the land power
and the sea power had fought themselves to a standstill. Yet
when the contest was shortly resumed the sea power, though
still supreme in its element, did not fight again on equal terms
until ten more years had passed and the land itself had risen
against its oppressor. The most obvious defects were the failure
to insist on the evacuation of the Netherlands and to exact a

commercial treaty. More serious still would have been to surrender to Bonaparte the command of the Mediterranean by letting Malta go as well as Minorca. This, at the risk of moral obloquy, Addington in the end refused to confirm.

(b) 1803-15

Britain soon discovered that her sacrifices had brought her few of the expected fruits of peace. Her merchants were exasperated to find their goods shut out from continental and colonial markets which the war had opened to them. In Germany and Italy, France continued her advance. Misgivings over the activity of French agents in the Eastern Mediterranean seemed confirmed when, on 30 January 1803, the publication of Sebastiani's notorious Report drew attention to the ease with which Egypt might be retaken. When Britain requested compensation for the extension of French power since the Treaty, Bonaparte took his stand upon the Treaty itself. He refused to admit that she had any right to interfere in the affairs of the Continent, least of all in the interpretation of his treaty with Austria to which the changes related. Lord Hawkesbury replied that Britain would never forgo her right of interfering "on every occasion in which her interests or those of Europe appeared to require it". Our national naïveté was seldom better illustrated than in our ambassador's argument that "by our possession of Malta France was not threatened; but the reverse was the case should the access to Egypt be opened by its evacuation".

In the final exchange of notes Britain made it clear that nothing would now satisfy her short of the evacuation of Holland and such security for Malta as her own continued occupation would give her. Bonaparte, consistently, declined to admit discussion outside the question of Malta. If that island were to go to Britain, he insisted, then France would have to be compensated, say with Otranto. This being regarded as a mere delaying tactic to give time for some French colonial expeditions to leave the high seas, the British ambassador asked for his passports. Unluckily, he thereby overrode a belated Russian effort at mediation, and so gave offence to the Tsar. In thus forcing an issue over Malta Britain threw away much of the moral advantage which Bonaparte's aggressions had given her. Once French *bona fides* became suspect the enormity of the sacrifice of that strategic island had been driven home to the Government. As Castlereagh put it, the issue in fact was "the effectual establishment of the British power in the Mediterranean".

Meanwhile, in Malta itself, the British minister, Sir Alexander Ball, had been holding a precarious balance between French and Neapolitans clamouring for him to get out, and British and Maltese beseeching him to stay. As the Government's efforts to find an acceptable Grand Master and to arrange the Six Power Guarantee grew more and more perfunctory, Ball felt increasingly embarrassed. Nevertheless, he held his head high and even managed to add to his reputation with the mass of the people.

The day war was declared (18 May 1803) Nelson was sent in a frigate to take up the Mediterranean command. In that sea which he knew so well there was now, apart from Malta, scarcely a friendly port, and it was imperative to protect the trade. Along the coasts of Spain and Italy lurked enemy privateers, seeking their prey where the seas narrowed, about the Gut of Gibraltar, and off the Calabrian and Tunisian coasts. Nelson organized regular convoys to be shepherded through danger zones by escorts centred on Gibraltar and Malta. Malta, indeed, though quite unsuited for the watch on Toulon— "When I am forced to send a ship there, I never see her under two months"—became the pivot of all operations east of Tunis. Detachments from it patrolled Sicilian and Ionian waters and kept an eye on French activity suggesting movement eastward.

Nelson himself watched Toulon with half a dozen heavy ships, dispersing the rest, with his frigate support, on the many lesser tasks. Unlike his predecessors, he declared his system "the very contrary of blockading". Watched distantly by a single frigate, the enemy was given every inducement to put to sea. Nelson avoided the old delays over watering and victualling by bringing the storeships up to the fleet and taking on at sea or in an unfrequented roadstead. For nearly two years his fleet did not enter a port. Yet, when the moment came, such had been his care for it, a violent chase of four thousand miles proved well within its powers.

Napoleon's aim was the landsman's, to conquer England by direct invasion with the army of Boulogne. His other moves were either feints or designed to close the coasts to British commerce. Apart from measures to safeguard the Channel and secure the East, Britain's only reply was to begin the recapture of the colonies she had so recently returned, and to extend the blockade. Where Napoleon was, accordingly, obliged to reorganize the economy of Europe, Britain united the resources of the tropics with her own industrial skill to vitiate the patterns he imposed. Colonial coffee, sugar and cotton, British cloth and hardware could not be kept out. Excluded from the Mediterranean coastline by Napoleon's military tentacles, goods which had formerly passed through Italian and Adriatic ports were now diverted through Denmark and Prussia to reach the same destination at an inflated cost. Gradually, too, new channels of supply began to open within the Mediterranean itself. Goods were run in from Malta through Sicilian and Neapolitan ports up the Adriatic to Trieste and Venice, or by way of the Russian-protected Ionians, Albania and Greece.

It was this growing interest in the Adriatic that brought Britain and Russia into uneasy contact during 1804 and led eventually to the Third Coalition. By the Convention of March 1800 Russia and Turkey had formed the Ionian Islands into the Septinsular Republic under their joint protection. The omission of Britain from this arrangement caused resentment among the currant traders, led by her devoted consul, Spiridion Foresti, while class and racial cleavage and island separatism made a breakdown inevitable. So when Ali of Janina, carving out for himself a private empire in and around Epirus, appeared about to invade the islands on behalf of the Porte, Russia seized the opportunity to reconstitute the Republic in her own interest, and become virtually an Adriatic power. One consequence of this was the Novosiltsoff mission to London in the autumn of 1804 with a scheme for a European settlement, hints of a partition of the Turkish Empire, and proposals for co-operation in the defence of Naples and Sicily.

Meantime, in May 1804, Napoleon had been proclaimed

Emperor, Pitt succeeded Addington, and the tempo of the war increased. Determined to end a state of affairs where French marauders used Spanish ports with impunity, Pitt provoked a rupture with Spain, and then forwarded to the Mediterranean a military expedition which he had promised the Tsar. For Napoleon the opportunity at last presented itself of marshalling the combined navies in the grand eighteenth-century manner for the conclusive assault on Britain which had so far exceeded his powers.

Pitt's next step was to complete the *rapprochement* with Russia until now held up by the Tsar's insistence on being given Malta. It was on 19 January 1805 that he laid down the ground plan of the Europe that was eventually to emerge through the work of his disciple Castlereagh. In the south of Europe it followed traditional lines, restoring and strengthening Sardinia as a barrier against France, extending Austrian power in Italy, and securing Neapolitan independence. Over Malta, however, Pitt was reluctant to compromise, though in June he made a half-hearted offer to consider an exchange for Minorca. In the end it was Napoleon himself who goaded the Tsar into agreement by annexing Genoa and assuming the throne of Italy in defiance of the Peace of Lunéville. On 28 July 1805 the Anglo-Russian Treaty was ratified, and on 9 August Austria gave her adherence to this Third Coalition.

Napoleon's scheme for the invasion of England derived from his belief that by a concentrated attack on the West Indies he could so endanger Britain's financial security that Pitt would be forced to divert the Navy there and leave the Channel open. A preliminary raid by the Rochefort fleet was to be followed up in the spring of 1805 by the combined effort of four more fleets. In the end, only three of the four got away. Thinking to confront Britain with a choice between immediate conquest or slow ruin, Napoleon succeeded only in baffling his own admirals. Poised at Martinique awaiting the fleet from Brest, they could neither persevere with the West Indian war nor, with their inadequate numbers, return and risk the issue in the Channel which was to release the Boulogne flotilla.

At the end of March 1805 Villeneuve, eluding Nelson, slipped out of Toulon with nineteen sail. Bound by his instruc-

tions, Nelson had no alternative but to maintain his watch on
Sicily and the central Mediterranean. Three weeks passed
before he learned that the French had passed out of the Straits
and been joined by the Spanish from Cadiz. Assuming their
object to be either Ireland or the Channel, he started in pursuit,
preparing to link up with the other fleets in defence of the
Western Approaches. In the teeth of contrary winds he beat his
way to Gibraltar in a fortnight, there to seek further news.
Meanwhile, the fate of Pitt's "secret expedition" bound for
Malta appeared to be at stake. Leaving England in the middle
of April with 7,000 troops and 45 transports, General Craig
suddenly found the Cadiz blockade abandoned and the Mediterranean fleet "missing". He sidled into the Tagus and prepared
to seize the forts. Not till he heard of Nelson's arrival did he
proceed on his way.

Leaving the Mediterranean to his cruisers, Nelson now
risked giving chase to a fleet twice his strength which he
reckoned must have gone to Martinique. On 4 June he reached
Barbados, only, through a false report, to miss Villeneuve, who
thereupon raced back to Europe with a four days' lead. After a
skirmish with Calder on 22 July Villeneuve entered Ferrol on
2 August. A fortnight earlier Nelson reached the Straits.
Finding no trace, he revictualled at Tetuan and plunged north-
ward as he had originally intended. But Villeneuve, daunted
by the fleets massing between himself and Boulogne, suddenly
turned about and ran for Cadiz in accordance with an earlier
instruction.

To the last minute the Emperor waited at Boulogne. Then,
hearing of his admiral's flight, he turned furiously upon the
armies preparing against him in central Europe under the
shelter of the naval war. If England could not be conquered by
way of the sea, he believed she might by the more circuitous
way of the land. He launched his offensives, therefore, east and
south. Craig had reached Malta in July. Naples, assured of
Anglo-Russian assistance, asked for the withdrawal of the
French garrisons. While he himself marched on the upper
Danube, therefore, Napoleon ordered Villeneuve's thirty-six
sail, their commander superseded, to re-enter the Mediterranean and take on reinforcements for the army of Calabria.

but he himself again retired to Sicily at the end of July and for six more crucial weeks refused to budge. Not until 23 September, when the Austrians had all but concluded peace, did he at length spare 1,800 men under Brigadier Oswald for an attack on Zante and Cephalonia.

These islands, together with Ithaca and Cerigo, fell easily during the first fortnight of October and, urged on by Leake and the ambassador at the Porte, Oswald would have pushed on to attempt Corfu as well. But Stuart was unwilling to get involved in so serious an undertaking while the defence of Sicily remained uncertain and ministers seemed uninterested. Even without Corfu, however, the move was opportune. For the defeat of Austria gave France the east coast of the Adriatic as far down as Scutari and, with Russia attacking on the Danube, opened up anew the danger of Turkish partition.

Meanwhile, Britain was becoming absorbed in the Spanish Peninsula. In the summer of 1809, Wellesley won the grim victory of Talavera on the upper Tagus and then withdrew to his lines at Torres Vedras. To this success the garrison of Gibraltar contributed by rushing a reinforcement into Cadiz when Marshal Soult was advancing on it early that spring. Henceforward, lacking command of the sea, the French were to find themselves as helpless in the marshes around Cadiz as on the barren waste in front of Wellington's lines.

The Allies now set themselves to wear down the armies of Napoleon's marshals, the Spanish by guerrilla fighting, the British through sea power. The Spanish strove heroically to keep their hold on the east coast fortresses, and supported by the fleet and by arms from Gibraltar, kept the French marching breathlessly up and down the coast. In October 1809 Collingwood retrieved an earlier lapse by cutting off a relieving squadron from Toulon and burning its convoy in the Bay of Rosas. Gibraltar became an arsenal for guerrillas everywhere. For the first time in its history the fortress was allowed a special naval establishment—a dozen gunboats—to keep enemy privateers in check and assist the coastal operations. Algeçiras Island, Ceuta and Tarifa were successively occupied during the spring of 1810 and, with the Junta's hesitant approval, the Spanish lines on the Isthmus gleefully demolished. General Campbell gathered round him a little empire of the Straits. The question was even raised whether Gibraltar or Cadiz might not prove a better operational base than Lisbon. But Wellington was well content to have over a third of the French army tied down in the south.

As Wellington's campaign developed during 1810 and 1811 the threat on the southern flank and the drain of manpower sapped his opponent's effort. When Soult moved off in December 1810 to go to Masséna's assistance, General Graham landed from the sea at Algeçiras to snatch the bloody victory of Barrosa, half-way between Gibraltar and Cadiz. Next year Soult tried in vain to put down the resistance in his rear, for whenever the Spanish General Ballesteros was pressed he retired snugly under Gibraltar's guns. Tarifa, like Cadiz, was held from the sea, denying the French access to Morocco.

In planning the campaign of 1812 Wellington reckoned on an east coast diversion by a force from Sicily, which had meanwhile survived another invasion threat. Between June and September 1810 Murat had concentrated 500 gunboats and 25,000 men, double Stuart's strength, at invasion sites between Scilla and Reggio. As the naval protection could not operate effectively in such narrow waters, it was feared that the Toulon fleet might escape and come up in support. A landing was actually made on 17 September seven miles south of Messina, but so severely was it dealt with that Murat suddenly called off the entire enterprise. By the middle of 1812, therefore, Lord William Bentinck, Stuart's successor, having calmed a domestic crisis, was free to lend assistance in Spain.

Bentinck's contingent arrived too late to create the diversion desired by Wellington but, nevertheless, when King Joseph retired on Valencia after the defeat of Salamanca he found the Sicilian force uncomfortably near at Alicante. As Soult now raised the siege of Cadiz and marched to join Joseph in a new advance on Madrid, Spain, south of the Tagus, was left free of regular French occupation. That winter Wellington was forced back from Burgos as far as Ciudad Rodrigo in a chaotic retreat. But at the same time Napoleon's own great army of the east was disintegrating in a yet more terrible retreat through the snows of Russia and Poland.

By the march into Russia, indeed, Napoleon had confessed

the breakdown of the system of Tilsit and the imminent collapse of the order which, as a result of Trafalgar, he had been forced to impose on Europe. In the great war of attrition England had saved herself, and now other nations were preparing to follow her lead. Excluded from the shores of northern Europe Britain had extended her hold on the Tropics and returned to the Mediterranean. She had developed the method of the *entrepôt* and the differential technique of the licence. Through Lisbon and Cadiz she had tapped both Spain and the Indies. From her warehouses in Gibraltar and Malta her merchandise filtered in through every crevice in the Emperor's coastal system, expanding the volume of her exports and buttressing her finances by reducing the drain of specie for her fleets and armies. The defence of Sicily covered Malta. The capture of the Ionians screened Turkey and opened up a hundred pores into central Europe. Peace with Turkey (January 1809) opened up the route of the Danube and provided Egyptian grain for the Peninsula armies when the American supply was cut off. By methods such as these an island of business men instinctively harnessed sea, plantation and factory to overthrow a continent planned for war.

Behind and conditioning these developments lay the steady influence of sea power. Collingwood died, worn out, on the eve of the taking of Sta Maura (March 1810). He had commanded one of the greatest single fleets that his country had ever commissioned and borne the diplomatic responsibility for the whole Mediterranean for more than four years. In the heyday of uninhibited imperialism he had quietly eschewed *raison d'état*, and insisted on the honouring of obligations even with those who, like the States of Barbary, were reputed to break theirs. He seemed irreplaceable. Yet after his death Cotton and Pellew kept Toulon no less tightly blockaded. There was now little action for battle fleets, but for frigate commanders like William Hoste of the *Amphion* it was an age of buccaneering splendour. Capturing convoys, sacking towns and fortresses, shelling roads and the armies on them, fighting regular actions against odds, it was among small detachments battling for prizes on the coasts of Spain, Italy and Greece that the spirit of Nelson lived on.

In the spring of 1813 the structure of Napoleonic Europe
was still standing. The Emperor, back in Paris, was raising new
armies by the magic of his name. In the north his garrisons
and the now friendly winter kept the Russians at bay behind
the Vistula. On Britain the war with the United States, declared
in June 1812, was beginning to impose a heavy strain not only
in men and ships but on her lifelines of food and trade. It was
half perceived that this year or the next would be decisive for
victory or stalemate. In the steps of Pitt his master, Castlereagh,
began building a last Coalition about the ruins of the Grand
Army. Wellington, who had recouped quietly on the Douro,
began making ready to advance once more, this time to the
Pyrenees. Away in the south the Whig Bentinck was preparing
grandly to liberate Italy.

It was late in May 1813 before Wellington judged the season
ripe for his great effort. Once again he reckoned on an effective
east coast diversion. He himself pushed rapidly across northern
Spain in a broad outflanking movement, which prevented
Joseph from gathering in his forces before being brought to
battle beyond the Ebro, on 21 June, at Vittoria. But having
won that great victory Wellington found his own flank threatened
by Marshal Suchet, to whom the route of the Ebro had been
left open by the Eastern Army's sluggishness, and the campaign
was temporarily halted at the walls of San Sebastian.

Before this, however, the Emperor had been dealt such blows
in Germany that he escaped with difficulty across the Rhine.
Murat rushed back to save his kingdom from Bentinck. In the
Adriatic British naval forces drew tighter the blockade of
Corfu and continued a fine series of operations which, beginning
with Hoste's brilliant frigate action off Lissa in March 1811,
only ended with the same officer's scaling of the mountain
citadels of Cattaro and Ragusa in the winter of 1813-14.

By the end of the year France was everywhere hemmed in
except on the Italian front, where Eugène Beauharnais was
holding the lines of the Po and Adige. Genoa had fallen to
Bentinck. On 11 January 1814 Austria, with Castlereagh's
approval, made a separate peace with Murat to enable them to
join forces against Eugène and, with Bentinck, co-operate in an
invasion of France from the south. By this treaty Murat was

promised Naples in return for his guaranteeing Sicily to
Ferdinand. By the end of the month he was in Bologna, with
Italian hopes of liberation gathering about his person and all to
the south controlled by his troops. Bentinck, however, stood out.
He refused to accede to such a treaty. Instead, he landed at
Leghorn, himself called upon Italians to rise for their freedom,
and put every obstacle in Murat's path. Consequently, instead
of the Allies in the south playing their part in the events of
February and March 1814 as Wellington did in the south-west,
they made no impression on Eugène's skilful resistance, which
was maintained until after Napoleon's abdication on 6 April.
In the Adriatic, similarly, Parga was occupied in March to
protect the inhabitants from Ali, but Corfu did not surrender
till 21 June.

Many of the outlines of the final settlement had already been
drawn by the Allies in the course of marshalling Europe against
Napoleon. Castlereagh followed Pitt in his insistence on security
against further French aggression. In Italy, therefore, he agreed
to strengthen Austria by giving her Venice as well as Lombardy
and, virtually, Tuscany and Modena as well; to subject Genoa
to the more reliable Sardinia; and, generally, to restore the
legitimate monarchs as a pledge against a revival of Jacobinism.

In the case of Naples the restoration of Ferdinand was less
assured, because of his character and of Austria's commitment
to Murat. Had it not been for Bentinck's irresponsible refusal
to sign, Britain would have been equally committed. Murat's
standing as a Liberal and his revolutionary past, however, made
him suspect to both powers. They had secretly agreed to overthrow him when, on Napoleon's return from Elba, he played
into their hands by a reckless second attempt to unite Italy
under his banner. In May 1815 he was routed and fled to
France. Napoleon refused to employ him. In October 1815,
three months after Waterloo, he made a desperate landing on
the coast of Calabria and was there speedily taken and executed.
Ferdinand being reinstated and the British troops withdrawn,
the old order was soon restored. Bentinck's Tory successor,
A'Court, approved the pledge to Austria not to introduce a
constitution in Naples without her consent.

G

In Spain the Liberal regime was even more speedily an
completely overthrown. Ferdinand VII withdrew the Constitu
tion of 1812 and began a reign of terror which soon engulfe
many of the leaders of the War of Liberation. The Sout
American trade remained officially closed. Britain had to b
content with a Treaty of Alliance promising her most favoure
nation treatment and abandoning the Family Compact.

Malta became British in full sovereignty. The Tsar ha
given up his claim in July 1812 in order to get British help, an
Ferdinand of Naples was in no position to assert his suzerainty
The Knights of St. John, though represented at the Congress c
Vienna, were in practice ignored. So just at the moment wher
owing to the imminent disruption of the outlying provinces c
Turkey, the Eastern Question was about to assume its mos
urgent aspect, Britain confirmed her hold on the finest nava
base in the world. Valletta combined the advantages of Gibralta
and Port Mahon. Like the former it was invulnerable by se
and by land. Like the latter it possessed an excellent harbou
which was, moreover, as Mahon's was not, safe from the land
ward side. By holding Malta Britain commanded the centra
narrows, cut off France from the Levant and Egypt, and looke
out over the Ionian and Aegean seas.

This strong position was reinforced by the virtual acquisitio
of the Ionian Islands. At first, Britain had not wanted them fo
herself. As with the Maltese before the Peace of Amiens, how
ever, she recognized an obligation to the inhabitants. She wa
determined, moreover, for strategic reasons that Corfu shoul
not pass again to France or Russia. So Castlereagh merely kep
the islands in reserve, as a bargaining counter, intending to offe
them to the King of Naples, if Murat should keep his kingdom
or else to Austria as heir to Venice. This latter proposal bein
turned down by the Tsar in April 1815, the matter was left ove
during the Hundred Days. By that time the gathering weight o
informed opinion, strategic and commercial, inclined Britai
at last to keep the islands herself. The Tsar's special representa
tive on the question, Capodistrias, himself an Ionian, suggeste
that the British Parliament's vigilance would be the best of al
guarantees of the islanders' liberty.

It came as a surprise, therefore, in September, when th

Tsar "regretted" he could only offer a protectorate to Britain, because of *his* obligation to a people whom he had been forced to sacrifice at Tilsit. Capodistrias reminded Castlereagh of Britain's original promise. To soften the blow, however, he argued that in effect, "nominal protection might mean actual sovereignty, varying only the designation of the government and the mode of acting". Though this was less satisfactory than Britain had hoped, she was by now too convinced of the value of the islands to be willing to forgo them, and accepted the protectorate on terms defined in a Treaty of 5 November 1815. The guarantors were Britain herself, Austria, Russia and Prussia.

CHAPTER VI

EXPERIMENTS IN GOVERNMENT, 1783–1815: CORSICA, MINORCA, MALTA, GIBRALTAR, IONIAN ISLANDS, SICILY

Corsica

THE possessions acquired by Britain during the Great War with France stood together as a group presenting similar problems. Their peoples had much in common with the Minorquins, being Roman Catholics, socially and economically somewhat retarded, and culturally proud and self-contained. The first acquisition was Corsica, and there it was natural for ministers to follow the rule-of-thumb approach familiar in Minorca.

The Corsicans were institutionally more advanced than the Minorquins, having, under different names, all the apparatus of an independent republic, from the elected village councils at the bottom to the parliament and president at the top. Socially, however, they were hardly suited for organized democracy. Essentially highland clansmen with loyalties primarily to the family or the village, they were only capable of combining in an hour of extremity. A pastoral, even a hunting people, theirs was the home of the *maquis* and the *vendetta*. Liberty, indeed, they prized, but it was of a private rather than a public kind. Economically, moreover, they had only the simplest wants and union with a great empire could have for them only a fleeting appeal.

Their leader, Paoli, was already famous for his heroic resistance to the French and had been lionized in English society by Boswell, whose *Account of Corsica* appeared in 1768. Inspired by him they *viva'd* their English liberators and trailed in their thousands to the fastness capital at Corte to acclaim the connection. The rest was anti-climax. They rode back with their long guns to their mountain hamlets, and the year was scarcely out before they were resisting the tax-collector in the age-old manner and demonstrating the futility of juries where a single conviction would start twelve more murderous feuds.

This character was not understood by the British architects of the union, Henry Dundas and Sir Gilbert Elliot. Both men thought like Paoli in terms of contemporary Ireland. Dundas was even willing to cement the union on terms which would give the island complete independence except for trade and foreign affairs. Even these were "not . . . indispensably to be insisted upon".

In the Constitution finally approved by the Corsican Consulta in June 1794, a strong executive authority was vested in the Viceroy, with command of the Army and certain safeguards for the Imperial interest in the form of veto, pardon, and control of appointments. Legislation and finance were left to the Corsican Parliament, which was to be a single House elected on a broad property franchise and modelled on the House of Commons. The islanders were to have their own flag and the same protection for trade and navigation as other British subjects. On the surface, it was just such a union as, Elliot assured Paoli, would join the two nations under a common sovereign and "at the same time secure for ever the independence of Corsica, and the preservation of her own ancient Constitution, laws and religion".

These were liberal imperial sentiments, but they could hardly be realized in the atmosphere of that time. The Corsican experiment foundered on the rock of executive responsibility; for the day had not yet come when the Crown could contemplate exercising its executive functions on the advice of ministers not ultimately responsible to the British Parliament. Otherwise conditions were favourable for the emergence of a rudimentary Dominion. Though Elliot sensed the nature of the problem he could not go further than consult his "private council", while not necessarily taking its advice. Paoli, on the other hand, when he proclaimed the British Constitution as his model, meant just what he said. Corsica would not be content with the eighteenth-century colonial system.

The weaknesses in these arrangements were soon apparent. In forming his Council Elliot tried to balance British and

Corsican interests, but the tardy arrival of Frederick North, the English Secretary of State, allowed power to fall into the hands of Pozzo di Borgo, the President of the Council. Pozzo was Paoli's own protégé and Elliot's close friend, but when it was seen that Paoli had been passed over for president as he had been for viceroy, a Paolist party formed against him both in and out of Parliament. Equally serious was Elliot's dispute with General Charles Stuart over the command of the armed forces in the island. Stuart's commission specified all troops in the Mediterranean area, and when he left in pique, the feud was inherited by John Moore, Oakes and other officers. As affairs on the Continent opposite grew steadily more threatening, rumours of the Army's disloyalty spread among the people and it became clear there could be no peace while Moore and Paoli remained. Moore was accordingly recalled and Paoli retired to England with an ample pension, in October 1795. For a time there was quiet; but all this played its part in alienating Corsican affections.

Although the government passed much legislation of constructive value, by the time the second Parliament met, in November 1795, ominous cracks were appearing in the administrative structure. In more isolated regions resistance to tax-collection was taking the form of armed clashes with the troops, and one of Parliament's first steps was to abolish the jury system which, being quite unworkable, was encouraging acts of violence.

In April 1796 organized rebellion broke out at Bocognano, cutting the main route between Corte and Ajaccio. Coinciding with Bonaparte's victories in north Italy, this marked the beginning of the end. His own tepid nominee, General Trigge, resigning rather than commit his troops to a punitive expedition against such skilled guerilla fighters, Elliot was left helpless for more than a month.

When at last an expedition did set out, Elliot accompanied it and, to the dismay of his subordinates, purchased success by conceding every insurgent demand. Taxes were remitted, an amnesty granted. Pozzo di Borgo and all the Viceroy's most trusted advisers in the Council were obliged to resign. The price of this eleventh-hour admission of a measure of ministerial responsibility, however, consisted in Britain's shouldering the entire cost of the administration.

A respite was gained. But by the end of June Bonaparte's advance guard was in Leghorn and Republican emissaries were landing in the island. For a moment ranks joined, as the ancestral spirit of resistance rallied the island against the invader. Elliot's own spirit was beginning to rise when, at the end of September, he received orders to evacuate the island and read the Government's laboured excuses for leaving the Corsicans to their fate. After that, it was with his tacit approval that, to avoid victimization, contact was made with Leghorn and committees set up to preserve order. Nelson watched over the evacuation of the troops to Elba in the third week of October, while Elliot arranged pensions for Pozzo and others and made provision for many refugees.

Minorca

The experience in Corsica was not lost on either Dundas or General Stuart when they came in 1798 to direct the re-occupation of Minorca. This time Dundas merely stipulated that economy should be observed and the attachment of the inhabitants secured "by conferring on them all the advantages of efficient protection under a mild and paternal government". A preliminary study of the official correspondence had warned Stuart of the "wranglings and disagreements" of former occupations. Shrewdly, therefore, in the Capitulations of 15 November 1798 he contrived not to commit the British Government at all with regard to religion, property rights or political privileges.

Without loss of time Stuart proceeded to set up what he took care to insist was merely a provisional government. Existing institutions and functionaries were maintained while he investigated the financial, judicial and religious arrangements. Inquiry revealed the benefits bestowed by the recent Spanish administration. It was along the lines of just such a benevolent despotism that Stuart meant to go.

The Universities were his toughest problem. He freed them from dependence on Ciudadella and staffed them with new officers under a revised electoral procedure. Their accounts he laid open to public inspection. To foster public spirit, he insisted, like Murray, that the Jurats should be men of property serving like English J.P.s without fees or other emoluments. A general reform of the finances, including the removal of the clerical immunity, reduced the burden of taxation and enabled a sinking fund to be established. In the public service many useless places were abolished, but those which remained were paid more highly.

Reforms such as these left the fabric of Minorquin institutions unaltered and did the minimum of violence to local sentiment. At the same time, coming from above, they removed the pretence of self-government and closed a number of channels through which opposition had formerly been directed. Stuart's successors bore witness to their good effect.

In one important respect, however, a change had been introduced by the Spanish which was full of danger for the new administration. In 1795 Minorca had been reconstituted an episcopal see, and Don Antonio Vila y Campo had been appointed the first bishop. At first Stuart proceeded circumspectly, but the Bishop's reluctance to accept his terms— dependence on Rome direct instead of *via* Spain, and jurisdiction only in spirituals and under government supervision— provoked him into a too imperious tone. Offended, Vila y Campo thenceforward resisted all attempts to limit his claims. He admitted clergy without the Governor's sanction, forbade them to pay taxes, and heard civil causes in the Ecclesiastical Court. When in April 1800 General Fox, exasperated beyond measure, suspended him from his functions, he began a systematic intimidation of state officials, threatening them with excommunication.

Resistance to the administration, denied expression through constitutional channels, now rallied round the Bishop. The entire population was soon on edge and there was danger of civil government breaking down. General Fox noted that the Bishop's behaviour was always more violent when enemy fleets appeared superior in the Mediterranean. In July 1801 the Bishop received permission to lay his case before the King, and the last straw, in Fox's eyes, was the levy of a popular contribution to pay his expenses. No settlement of this issue was ever attempted, however, because the island was shortly returned to Spain.

During this Third British Occupation Minorca showed no development economically, and its military and naval limitations were confirmed. St. Philip's Castle having been wisely demolished by the Spanish, Stuart merely devised a scheme of elastic defence to delay an invader until help could arrive by sea. The Navy remained the primary defence, and until the acquisition of Malta the island continued an undue preoccupation of naval commanders. Not lightly did Nelson complain of Lord Keith's obsession with its safety. A first article in the naval commander-in-chief's instructions, it tended to paralyse the offensive operations farther up the Mediterranean which alone promoted the war. Unlike Gibraltar or Malta it could not be relied upon to withstand a prolonged siege. More so than the other fortresses it was dependent on the Navy rather than the Navy on it.

Malta

The next islands to come under British rule were Malta, Gozo and Comino, whose capital and great port Valletta was surrendered by General Vaubois in September 1800. Together they covered 118 square miles (Malta 91) and their population was rather more than 100,000.

Lying midway between the Straits of Gibraltar and Egypt and commanding the central narrows where Italy stretches down towards North Africa, Malta's history has been stormy. In 1530 the Emperor Charles V granted the islands to the Knights of the Order of St. John of Jerusalem recently driven out of Rhodes by Suleiman the Magnificent. A condition of the award was the reversion of Malta to the King of Sicily, as suzerain, if ever the Order abandoned its trust. The Maltese inhabitants were ignored. They had to make the best terms they could with the new rulers, and were given a promise that their property, laws and usages would be respected. At the time they were said to number about 15,000, to live in terror of the corsairs, and to extract their living from the bare rock.

Until 1798 Malta's history was that of the Knights who, after holding out gloriously against the Turks in 1565, gradually declined in vigour and importance until they were chiefly renowned for their hospital and lazaretto. The wonderful fortress-port of Valletta, rising steeply on its peninsula from the wharves of its twin harbour, its entrance like the vestibule, its streets like the staircases of some huge white mansion, was their creation. Under their rule the people of Malta multiplied, and by importing new soil and using what they had to advantage, converted their rocky island into the congeries of fertile walled fields and terraced gardens which, behind the façade of stone, it still is today—that "noble memorial to human industry" which the Commissioners of 1812 described.

However, like other subject peoples, the Maltese grew discontented politically as their economic prospects rose, and by the time of the French Revolution there were spirits among them ready to strike out for independence—at any rate of the Knights. When, therefore, on 9 June 1798, Bonaparte paused on his way to Egypt, Grand Master Hompesch yielding Valletta without a struggle, the Maltese, in spite of some religious qualms, greeted the French as liberators.

But three months of government by decree, aimed at turning them from their "ignorance and superstition" into progressive Frenchmen, was more than they could stomach. On 2 September 1798, elated by word of Nelson's victory, they used an insult to their religion as excuse for revolt. The ancient red-and-white flag was raised, the French shut in Valletta, a representative body elected to guide the movement, and—on second thoughts—an appeal sent to the King of the Two Sicilies, to whom the sovereignty had reverted.

This was Britain's opportunity. While the Navy held the seas a small British force gave what help it could by land, and the French finally surrendered to it alone, neither the Maltese nor the Neapolitans being allowed to share in the Capitulation. This had not been the original intention. On 13 November 1798 the Tsar Paul had accepted the Grand Mastership of the Order, considered forfeit by Hompesch, and six weeks later, by a tripartite agreement, Russia, Britain and Naples had arranged to garrison the islands jointly until the Order could be restored. To this arrangement Britain adhered until the summer of 1800, when a rupture with Russia was in sight and there was danger from Russian forces gathered at Corfu and Naples. The King of Naples, though he had contributed little to the siege, naturally claimed the sovereignty and was hurt at Britain's stand. The Maltese, similarly, supported by Nelson's colleague, Captain Alexander Ball, who had become their "Governor" during the siege, strongly resented being left out of the Capitulation and denied Britain's right to assume authority over them merely on the strength of Valletta having fallen to her. At the same time, they welcomed the association with Britain, only wanting it to be on more equal terms. How then, was Britain to proceed?

Again it was Dundas with whom the decision lay. He was directing his campaign to drive the French out of Egypt, and Malta figured in his plans as a base for both the services. He instructed General Pigot, accordingly, to keep the Russians out, to conciliate the Maltese and give the impression that it was neither Britain's wish nor intention to let Russia interfere or to place them again under the Order of St. John. In the provisional military government he was as far as possible to use Ball's services in civil matters, and interfere only where absolutely necessary with the institutions, prejudices and habits of the people.

This was the Minorca formula again, and it is clear that Dundas now had hopes of acquiring Malta for Britain. Indeed, as reports reached Ministers from Ball, Abercromby and others giving details of the institutions and the commercial and strategic value of the island they could not fail to be impressed. To an Imperial Power predisposed to confer "all the advantages of efficient protection under a mild and paternal government" Malta must have seemed a godsend. Here was an island with every characteristic which in those days was considered most desirable in a colony. To crown all, the people were attached to the British interest and, it was mistakenly assumed, wanted no more constitutionally than to be given back their former despotism, provided only it be exercised benevolently.

To give effect to these ideas Lord Hobart, who succeeded Dundas in March 1801, sent out Charles Cameron with the title of Civil Commissioner to take over formally Ball's unofficial jurisdiction in civil affairs. He was to be subordinate to the Commanding Officer only in the last resort. Hobart's instructions merely elaborated those of Dundas. The appointment of William Eton to take charge of the lazaretto and the opening of Valletta as a free port were intended to develop the island's economic possibilities.

But the error was continued of assuming that the Maltese really wanted the restoration not of their medieval rights but of the very institutions which they had, in fact, rejected under the Knights. It was not long before Cameron was given evidence of the mistake. To the social turmoil resulting from the dispossession of the Knights and the hardships of the siege was added a growing resentment of "military government", which was how the Maltese interpreted the new régime. In such conditions the news that, by the Preliminaries of Peace, the Order was to be restored suggested a betrayal; and the Maltese, encouraged by Eton and other sympathizers, sent a delegation to England, declaring their resolve "not to submit to any other power than Great Britain, preferring otherwise to perish under the walls of their city if they could not maintain their independence".

Britain's *rapprochement* with Russia and her need to make peace with France made the Maltese case hopeless for the time being. Britain did what she could. Her determination to "meliorate" their condition under the restored Order put the Marquis of Cornwallis at a disadvantage in the negotiations at Amiens, nothing having been stipulated to that effect in the Preliminaries. Fortunately, the concessions thus purchased—a Maltese *langue* supported out of the local revenues, and a half share in the garrison and in government appointments—never had to be taken up.

Fear of Bonaparte's intentions and inability to find an Order to restore or six European powers willing to guarantee it, caused first delays and finally a refusal to hand the island over. Though Ball was sent out in June 1802 as Minister Plenipotentiary to arrange the transfer, he was instructed to insist on all the conditions being first fulfilled and to do his utmost to ensure popular attachment to Britain. Accordingly, when hostilities were resumed in May 1803, the Englishman whom the Maltese loved and who was best equipped to govern them was already in office. Nelson, on his arrival to take up the Mediterranean command, was impressed by their high spirits. "They hope sincerely," he wrote, "never to be separated from England."

Between 1803 and 1813 Malta was administered by civil commissioners with the tacit consent of the people and under circumstances which, as Lord Liverpool put it, bore "no analogy to any other instance in the modern history of this kingdom". Their powers were never defined and their government had to be carried on by "personal management", a compromise between Maltese interest and sentiment on the one hand and Britain's war needs on the other. This meant in practice that Sir Alexander Ball and Sir Hildebrand Oakes who followed him found themselves heir to the despotic authority of the later Grand Masters, and conducted the government on principles which the islanders had already condemned. Inevitably there was oppression and corruption. While the Civil Commissioner's reserve of power was regarded by some as the fount of mercy and justice, to others it seemed a "vast engine of corruption". Nor was a status of such dubious legality made easier to bear by the persistent criticisms of the "Eton faction" whose complaints more than once shook the Government's confidence in its representatives' integrity.

Grave as were the administrative difficulties, they were more than compensated for by the island's amazing economic progress which fully realized the dream of commercial empire. Even in normal times Malta offered remarkable facilities for trade, and its central position suited the sailing capacity of small vessels from every part of the Mediterranean. In war time it became the ideal rendezvous of the licensed trader and the smuggler, Briton and foreigner alike. Between the opening of the free port in November 1801 and 1806 British exports to Malta rose to a quarter of a million pounds.

The events of 1807-8 brought further leaps to three-quarters of a million and then three million pounds, reflecting the Government's plan to make Malta the central depot of Mediterranean trade and the general pressure of the Continental System and the American Embargo Act. Between 1808 and 1812 these conditions continued and trade settled down into fairly regular channels. French and English alike conspired to travesty the system of mutual blockade. Through Marseilles and Leghorn, Naples and Trieste, Scutari and Salonika, Patras, Smyrna and Constantinople, the civilized necessities were run in under any flag, with licenses printed in London and Paris. For Malta the terrible outbreak of plague in 1813 was an economic disaster.

Sir Alexander Ball died suddenly in October 1809 deeply regretted by the majority of the Maltese people. Even of temper, philosophic, indulgent, yet firm where need arose, he had been a father to them. His successor, Oakes, whom we saw in Corsica, was similarly mild of disposition but inevitably smaller in moral stature. Under him Maltese discontents again rose to the surface, excited still by Eton and led by members of the nobility whose fixed incomes put them at a disadvantage alongside commercial men.

Anxious to quiet this agitation and put the administration on a regular footing Lord Liverpool dismissed Eton and in May 1812 set up a Commission of three, including Oakes himself, to investigate the island's affairs. The findings of this Commission, incorporated in their General Report, provide the best information we have of Malta in this period. Their proposals, however, follow too closely the lines laid down in their instructions not to suggest some lack of sympathy with Maltese aspirations. They decided, in effect, for the system of government already worked out in the colonies conquered from Holland and Spain and applied instinctively by Stuart in Minorca— Crown Colony Government.

When Lord Liverpool became Prime Minister in May 1812 he was succeeded at the Colonial Office by Earl Bathurst, who was to hold that position for fifteen years and do much to shape the character of the new Empire. The following May the plague appeared and grew so serious as to carry off one in twenty of the population, ruin the finances and suspend all commerce. Oakes dealt with it vigorously but his own health was worn down and Bathurst took the opportunity to put in his place Lieutenant-General Sir Thomas Maitland who had won Ministers' confidence by his iron efficiency in Ceylon.

Maitland had little in common with men like Ball or Oakes. Starting life as a Foxite Whig, he believed he had learnt the error of his ways, and his experience in the East confirmed this impression. Self-confident, practical, untiring in pursuit of duty, he thrived on difficulties and welcomed the task which Malta offered. Yet, fundamentally, he looked down on the people whom he now came to govern, and even while he brow-beat them into orderly and honest citizens he felt hurt at the servility his attitude brought out. "I wish them to feel," he wrote, "that they have rights and privileges, and that as long as they keep themselves within these, that Government can have no interference with them." He was that Government.

After crediting himself with victory over the plague, Maitland went on to remodel the administration on the authori-tarian principles which his instructions laid down. As Governor and Commander-in-Chief he united the civil with the military power and surrounded himself with men who understood his ways. Instead of the Nominated Council recommended by the Commissioners, half Maltese and half British, Maitland allowed only officials, the Chief Secretary, the Treasurer, an auditor and assessor, whose functions were to do their own jobs efficiently. Beyond that, they might make suggestions, but hardly criticize.

The laws he left practically unaltered, except those relating to commerce, but he reorganized the courts and legal procedure. The Universita, or public corn corporation, he took out of the hands of the Jurats and made a department of government. He brought the finances under his own eye. He reduced the number of officials, but increased their pay and worked them harder. With Bathurst's support he endeavoured to retain for the island under peace conditions the commercial pre-eminence acquired during the war. Thus in 1815 Malta secured the same rights under the Navigation Acts as Leghorn and the other Privileged Ports, while a decision in 1817 to extend the range of goods which could be imported direct from the West Indies to Malta was also taken primarily in her interest.

This was of course good government, not self-government. In the Maitland-Bathurst dispensation there was no room for the Claims of the Maltese. It was a solution eminently suited to Malta in her character as fortress and *entrepôt*. But it could hardly be expected to satisfy for long a numerous and volatile people with high aspirations to determine their own destiny and good claims to do so. Nevertheless, under "King Tom", in spite of her deficiencies in temper, situation, resources and experience, Malta was being given a grounding for her journey towards self-determination.

Gibraltar

With the other great centre of Mediterranean power Lord Bathurst was better qualified to deal. Gibraltar's history during these years was surprisingly unwarlike. It was as if Eliott's resistance had not only proved it invulnerable but reconciled the Spanish to their loss. General Boyd died there in harness in 1794 at the age of eight-five, still quarrelling with the merchants about their civil rights and with Dundas about the guns and batteries. General O'Hara who succeeded him (1795-1802) was known affectionately as the Cock of the Rock. He added to the fortifications but under him the garrison exceeded its previous reputation for drunkenness. The Duke of Kent was sent out in 1802 to put this right, but his barrack-square methods only led to mutiny, so that he had to be recalled.

There were several visitations of the deadly Mediterranean fever, the worst in 1804 and 1813. In all, 15,000 people were attacked and half that number died. The fortress served its customary purpose as depot and information centre but was still neglected by the fleet, except for one period in 1799 when St. Vincent took his flag ashore and in 1801 when Saumarez effected his lightning repair there. Its pivotal position between the West Indies and the Mediterranean meant that the garrison was chronically undermanned, because of the temptation to draw on it when reinforcements were urgently needed for either area. The chief improvements were the construction of a *novia* for watering and the demolition of the Spanish Lines in 1809. It was in this period also that the Garrison Library and the Calpe Hunt were founded.

Nevertheless, Gibraltar rivalled even Malta in its contribution to Napoleon's downfall. The decline in trade which had resulted from General Bland's restrictions on smuggling had

H

been turned into an upward movement by the more accommo
dating attitude of General Eliott, so that in 1788 more than
£300,000 worth of British goods were being disposed of. The
crisis of Nootka Sound and the introduction of a Spanish consul
reduced the traffic once more, to the merchants' disgust, but at
length the artificial conditions of the trade war brought
similar boom to that in Malta.

Although less well placed for such commerce, Gibraltar had
in its favour long experience and established connections. No
sooner had the rupture with Spain cut the communication
across the Isthmus than small coastal vessels up to a hundred
a month, licensed by O'Hara and St. Vincent, were bringing in
wine and provisions and taking away great quantities of British
goods. The Berlin and Milan Decrees accelerated this activity.
Privateers from Gibraltar, equipped with letters of marque but
laden with merchandise, lay off the Andalusian coast discharg
ing their cargoes into the waiting Spanish boats, and fought of
the coastguards who tried to intercept them. Vessels from Cadiz
officially bound for Malaga or Barcelona, called in at Gibraltar
to take on goods already falsely cleared as from their port of
departure. The French Occupation only served to spur on these
activities. Exports from Britain to Gibraltar which had grown
to over £750,000 by 1807, reached £1,370,000 the next year
and in 1812 a peak of £2,420,000.

This great growth of trade was accompanied by a rise in the
civil population to upwards of 12,000, three-quarters of them
foreigners, and by its emphasis on mercantile pursuits brough
to a head the problems which the 1752 Charter had left unsettled.
A ceaseless struggle went on between the Governor and the
merchants led by the Judge-Advocate, Richard Jephson
Jephson chafed at his ambiguous status, but maintained the
law's defective processes against successive governors year after
year until, worn out, he retired to England in 1812 to advise on
new judicial establishment and receive a knighthood.

Lord Liverpool had considered sending the Malta Commis
sioners to Gibraltar to inquire into the administration, but in the
end it was Lord Bathurst who worked out a solution. Jephson'
successor, Larpent, and the Governor, General George Don
assisted him.

The Charter which emerged in 1817 confirmed government
by decree but provided a more generous judicial establishment
with a separate Civil Judge. Adequate salaries replaced the
former dependence on fees. The old question of officers' liability
for debt was this time decided in their favour, the Solicitor-
General defending the *prima facie* denial of justice on the
ground that civilians ought never to have settled in a military
station if they were not ready to subordinate their liberties as
British subjects to the prior claims of security. A subsidiary
Order-in-Council conferred authority to levy rates and so made
possible General Don's great work of renovation.

At last the administration of Gibraltar the fortress was being
given priority over Gibraltar the *entrepôt*, but at the same time
sufficient concessions were allowed to civilians to make life
more than tolerable for them there.

The Ionian Islands

Britain's administration of the Ionian Islands had much in
common with that in Malta, both because of the similarity of
social structure and because both came to bear the stamp of
"King Tom". The Seven Islands lie off the coast of Albania
and the Morea and are separated from the foot of Italy by the
Ionian Sea. They are rocky, beautiful islands with a climate and
aspect typically "mediterranean". They have numerous excellent
harbours; and Corfu was, and is, the Malta of the Adriatic.

The union with Venice, in spite of the disadvantages of
alien and monopolistic rule, had fostered the islanders' love of
seafaring and given them a symbolic status in the Greek world.
They were the Free Greeks. With Britain their connection
went back at least to the sixteenth century when the currants of
Corinth and Zante made their appearance in English plum
puddings. Their merchant shipping together with their
currants and olive oil enabled the islands to support a dense
population which numbered nearly 200,000 at the beginning
of the nineteenth century.

Socially, they were divided into classes on semi-feudal lines,
the old nobility, through whom the Venetians had ruled, forming
the traditional governing class. Mainly Roman Catholic, they

were linked with the West by their Italian speech and education and had little in common with the peasant cultivators on whose labour they lived. The peasants were Eastern in dress and manners, Greek in language, religion and sentiment. A third class, of capitalists, was also emerging, made up on the one hand of merchants desiring a closer connection with England, on the other of money-lenders into whose power the peasants were falling. Ionian institutions and customs closely resembled those of Corsica or Malta and included delight in litigation and the practice of the *vendetta*. The sudden influx of revolutionary ideas in 1797 converted them overnight into an enthusiastic "democracy".

Between the Peace of Campo-Formio and the British Occupation in 1809 the Ionian people went through a series of constitutional gyrations, passing from French into Russo-Turkish hands in 1799, being given nominal independence the following year as the Septinsular Republic, and after the Peace of Tilsit in 1807 returning quite thankfully to French control. As in Malta, however, efficient taxation proved irksome and, distressed for their vanished trade, the Zantiotes and Cephalonians led an appeal to Britain.

On receiving the surrender of the French garrisons, General Oswald was careful to explain that the British came only as "allies"; but he promised to re-establish a "free and independent government" with full religious, civil and commercial rights. Though the islanders made a great show of joy, it was noticed that they gave no active help. But at their request Oswald raised the British flag alongside the Septinsular one as token of British protection.

The next step was to form a stable administration. Having been instructed to limit military control as far as possible to general matters, Oswald set up a separate government in each island under a military officer with an advisory council. Local affairs continued to be dealt with through existing institutions. Gradually, however, a rudimentary central government came into existence to cope with assorted appeals and supervise revenue collection, and a Civil Secretary was appointed to take charge of these matters.

These arrangements worked far from smoothly in the face

of increasingly unruly faction, and in April 1811 the separate administrative bodies, largely representing the nobles, united to appoint Sr. Demetrio Foscardi to undertake a mission to London on behalf of the islands. Foscardi was so successful that in April 1812 Ionian commerce was granted the protection of the British flag and in October of the same year it was agreed to send out a Civil Commissioner on the Malta model. For this post it was important to find the right man.

Major-General James Campbell was not a very happy choice. A stern, earnest rather unimaginative man, he did not suit the Ionian temperament. His instructions, to avoid all but indispensable change, attach the people to Britain and consolidate British interests in Greece and the Adriatic, reflected the conservative and authoritarian trend already observed in Malta. The times, moreover, were peculiarly difficult. With the end of the war in sight every interest was elbowing for position. Campbell's forthright efforts to extract order out of anarchy only produced charges of a "reign of terror". Englishmen, it was said, talked much of their own liberty and justice, but "took very good care that nobody but themselves benefited by it".

He began badly. At the last minute the French had restored the extensive powers formerly held by the aristocratic Senate of Corfu, which now proposed to seek Russian support to re-establish the Septinsular republic. As it was quite unrepresentative of the other islands, Campbell refused to let it send an envoy to Vienna. In the end, Capodistrias, member of a leading Ionian family, did act for the islands, but as representative of the Tsar.

On the awkward question of Parga, Campbell did better. On the petition of the inhabitants his forces occupied the town in March 1814 just in time to save it from Ali of Janina, who was already in the outskirts. There being no doubt Ali had been promised possession, Britain was compromised from the start. But it was common humanity to keep him out and Britain's stock went up throughout the Hellenic world.

Under Foresti's influence, Campbell did what he could to encourage Ionian trade, and Zante and Argostoli were made free ports to absorb some of the produce being locked out of Malta because of the plague. But there were insufficient warehousing facilities and new channels of trade had no time to develop before the war ended. In 1814 trade between Britain and Ionia balanced at less than £50,000. As a commercial asset the islands really had little to recommend them.

His high opinion of Maitland's work in Malta persuaded Bathurst that he might do as well in Ionia. As early as August 1814, when annexation seemed assured, Bathurst planned to put Maitland in charge of all British Mediterranean affairs (apart from Gibraltar). The announcement of "protection" with conditions attached, reduced his enthusiasm, but he soon convinced himself that within the framework of the Treaty his favourite prescription might still be applied. And for this Maitland was the man. Maitland was accordingly asked, in December 1815, to take over from Campbell and report.

Sicily

Lord William Bentinck's constitutional experiment in Sicily must be mentioned at this point, though the story of it does not belong here, as the island never became British in spite of Bentinck's desire to make it so. Between 1811 and 1814 this headstrong son of the Whig Duke of Portland tried to make use of the large subsidy being paid to the King of Naples as a lever to force him to concede parliamentary reforms in the island, the inhabitants of which closely resembled the Corsicans and Ionians.

Bentinck hoped to free and perhaps unite Italy by presenting a reformed Sicily as an example which Italians would prefer to the Naples of Murat and rally round accordingly. The government of Lord Liverpool, however, had even less interest in constitutional reform abroad than it had at home. Its views were limited to providing the exiled king with a sufficiently contented realm to permit the English garrison to be reduced without danger to security. Once the military danger was removed, therefore, Bentinck received no more support for his schemes. The moment Murat was disposed of, the restoration of the former tyranny became a matter of course, and Sicilians were left with only a memory to rouse them in later days.

CHAPTER VII

THE MAINTENANCE OF SEA SUPREMACY, 1815-1900

THE triumph of 1815 was even greater than the one a century earlier, for this time the new Europe was almost precisely what Britain had fought to achieve. Castlereagh had carried out the plans of Pitt. Outside Europe the story was the same. Britain's unrivalled naval superiority, the strategic vantage points she had acquired, the commercial goodwill won in the process of undermining the Continental System assured her for years to come a monopoly of markets and raw materials. Nor would this privileged position be much resented, at any rate until European countries had solved their urgent internal problems and become industrialized in their turn. For Europe the nineteenth century was full of conflict, but for Britain it was the century of peace. Britain's wars were colonial ones and hardly noticed by people at home. The one apparent exception, the Crimean War, was, in fact, fought out in an Eastern pocket of the Mediterranean primarily to maintain this happy situation.

The story of Britain in the Western Mediterranean has, so far, been crowded with naval and military activity. In the nineteenth century this was no longer true. It was not because the Mediterranean had become a backwater; it was because, on the contrary, it was so dominated by Britain's naval power that nothing could take place on it or around its shores except with her consent. Great events took place. Greece was freed, Italy was united, France matured her North African empire. The Suez Canal opened a new artery of commerce between West and East. But in every case the Royal Navy gave its silent but essential approbation. In wanting to preserve the settlement she had made, Britain wanted peace; and in wanting peace she was bound, in the main, to want the things that made for peace. Whenever aspects of the settlement seemed incompatible with peace, Britain felt bound to alter the settlement in order to preserve or restore peace. Conservative or revolutionary as circumstances required she remained until the close of the century the decisive factor in Mediterranean affairs.

As the world's one wholly satisfied power, Britain was obliged in her foreign policy to reckon with two great social forces and two unsatisfied powers. The forces were those of Liberalism and Nationalism. Both were conspicuously products of the French Revolution and had for that reason been ignored in the Vienna Settlement. By Liberalism was meant government by the people themselves through their representatives as opposed to government by a despot or a privileged class. By Nationalism was meant that the area of government should be confined to people of similar language, culture and religion. In a Europe that included the Spain of Ferdinand VII, the France of the restored Bourbons, the Italy and Austria-Hungary of the Hapsburgs, and a Balkan peninsula ruled by the Turk, these were explosive forces, especially in the Mediterranean.

The two unsatisfied powers were defeated France and victorious Russia. Both abutted on the Mediterranean, France directly, with her commercial interests and traditional ambitions, Russia indirectly, in her search for a warm-water port. They both had aims which could hardly be realized without recourse to war. France was interested in Spain, Italy, North Africa, Egypt and the Levant; Russia in Balkan and Asiatic Turkey. Britain's route to the East was thus threatened at every step. It became, in effect, a frontier as well as a route; for by her care for it Britain was denying land-bound Europe its readiest access to the overseas world. The preservation of this frontier-route from the control of either Russia or France or a combination of both—there was the memory of Tilsit—constituted for Britain the so-called Eastern Question. Her anxiety to restrain the ambitions of these powers led her to meddle in the crises provoked by Liberal and Nationalist revolt.

The main lines of British foreign policy after 1815 were drawn by Castlereagh who remained Foreign Secretary until his suicide in 1822. Castlereagh had a personal interest in preserving his own creation. Under him Britain found herself participating in a system of congresses of the five Great Powers, meeting from time to time to discuss problems of common

oncern as they arose. Castlereagh was good European enough
o hold that Britain's interests went beyond the narrow bounds
f immediate national advantage; but he was not sufficiently
nternational-minded to satisfy the Tsar of Russia. Alexander
vas so determined to promote the principles of the Vienna
ettlement that he wanted to interfere in the home politics of
ther countries whenever these seemed likely to disturb those
rinciples. Consequently, the revolutionary outbreaks of 1820
nd 1821 in Spain, Italy and Greece brought the differences
etween Castlereagh and Alexander to a head, broke up the
ongress system and divided Europe on ideological lines.

Spain, Italy and Greece were the three peninsulas which
Napoleon had attempted to dominate as his means to Mediter-
anean and thence world power, and Britain was naturally
very interested in their fate. In Spain the revolution was a
iberal one, forcing Ferdinand to concede a constitution. The
Tsar interpreted this as a breach of principle and sought congressional permission to march an army across Europe to restore
he king; but in so drastic a course he did not even have the
upport of his friends in Berlin and Vienna, much less of Britain.
Castlereagh's State Paper of 5 May 1820 defined Britain's
attitude at the time and outlined it for the future. Britain would
not follow up ideas of "world government" or act upon "abstract
and speculative principles of precaution", it declared; but she
would be found in her place whenever actual danger threatened
he European equilibrium.

The upshot of the Spanish affair was, first, the intervention
of France to restore Ferdinand to his despotism; and then her
quiet withdrawal in 1827 in face of his ingratitude. During
that time Britain's armed guarantee of Portugal and the
Spanish colonies ensured that neither France nor Russia reaped
any advantage. Under the eye of the British Navy a breach of
Vienna principles had been repaired without endangering the
peace or affecting British interests.

Castlereagh's attitude was much the same in the case of
Italy, where revolutions occurred in Naples and Piedmont. As
Austria had been given special interests in the peninsula at
Vienna, he was willing that she should assume full responsibility
for restoring order. The Tsar again put his troops at the disposal

of the Congress powers. Neither Metternich nor Castlereagh would hear of their being used. But when Metternich insisted on getting congressional sanction for doing what he had a right to do under the Austro-Neapolitan Treaty of 12 June 1815, Castlereagh refused to be represented at the conference which met at Troppau in October 1820 to consider the matter. He denounced the interventionist principles which the conference proclaimed; but, nevertheless, he was gratified at the practical outcome, which gave Austria the required permission. By the close of 1821 the rebellions had been put down by Austrian troops and Austrian garrisons were quartered in most of the other Italian states. In Italy also the Vienna Settlement was maintained. The only question was whether it was not too high a price to pay for peace.

The Greek question yielded more readily to the anti-doctrinal approach. The issue there was national rather than liberal and it proved possible to divide congressional opinion by co-operating with the leading interventionist power. At first there was conflict between sentiment and interest, but in the end a typical British compromise was reached. The Greeks were, in part, freed, Turkish integrity otherwise maintained, and the Russians were still excluded from the Eastern Mediterranean.

In contrast to the British people the British Government was at first opposed to Hellenic aspirations. For commercial and strategic reasons Britain was impelled, in the Pitt tradition, to uphold the Porte's authority. This had already been Britain's attitude in the awkward case of Parga. By the terms of the Russo-Turkish Convention of March 1800 Parga and the other mainland dependencies of Venice had been ceded to Turkey. By the end of the Napoleonic Wars all except Parga had been occupied by Ali of Janina on behalf of the Porte. It was only the intervention of General Campbell in 1814 that saved Parga from a like fate. The Parguinotes were thankfully settling down under British protection, when they found to their dismay that Britain still admitted the Porte's claim. Offered an asylum in the Ionian Islands and some compensation for the loss of their homes, they regretfully accepted rather than brave the fury of the Pasha. Maitland received them well enough in Corfu in

1819; but the drastic whittling down of the compensation sum emphasized the shame of Britain's part in extinguishing the last free Greek community on the mainland. As at the same time, in London, Count Capodistrias was indicting Maitland's Ionian administration for perverting the letter and spirit of the Protectorate, Britain's name did not stand very high in the Hellenic world when the Greeks raised their flag at Patras.

Private Englishmen did something to restore the balance. The poetry of Byron and, even more, his death at Missolonghi blazoned the Greek cause before the peoples of Europe. Nearly three million pounds were raised for a Greek loan. Well-known Englishmen volunteered, and before the War of Independence ended were in command of the Greek forces by land and sea. But while the Greek cause was going well Canning's only step was, in March 1823, to admit their rights as belligerents. His object was simply to protect the Levant trade from Greek pirates. It was the intervention of Mehemet Ali of Egypt that transformed the situation.

Mehemet Ali was the Sultan's most powerful vassal. His navy was strong enough to wrest the command of the sea from the Greeks and by 1825 the savagery of his son Ibrahim threatened the Greeks of the Morea with extermination. By this time Alexander had died, and the new Tsar, Nicholas I, was less concerned with congressional principles. It seemed certain that he would go to the rescue of his co-religionists and in so doing violate Turkish integrity and advance Russian power to the Mediterranean.

Unable, in the circumstances, to defend the Turk Canning saw no alternative but to co-operate with Russia in the hope of thus restraining her. British sea power might provide a way to save the Greeks without violating Turkish soil. A measure of Greek independence having been agreed on, an Allied fleet under British command presented Ibrahim with an ultimatum imposing an armistice to which the Greeks had already agreed. Unfortunately, on 20 October 1827, a trivial misunderstanding in the Bay of Navarino led to the destruction of the combined Turkish and Egyptian fleets. By that time Canning was dead. Such interference was almost certainly farther than he had intended to go. Neverthleless, the independence of part of

Greece was now assured, and the Russian thrust parried.
British sea power had again decided a conflict of principle in the
Mediterranean without a general war.

While the eastern end of the Mediterranean frontier-route
was thus being taken care of, an event of great significance
occurred in the west. The other power chiefly feared by
Britain re-entered the colonial field, and did so in North Africa.
In July 1830 France occupied Algiers and laid the foundation
of her African Empire. To understand the circumstances of
this move it is necessary to go back a little way.

In the later years of the Peninsular War it became a British
practice to pay the Barbary States for their grain and meat in
the currency they preferred—arms and munitions. One result
was an increase of piracy. In 1815 Maitland of Malta was
resorted to—it was his own idea—and given control of all the
Barbary consuls except the Moroccan. His methods were
brusque but temporarily effective. Scorning etiquette, he went
off himself on a flying visit to Tunis, went straight to the palace
and scolded the Bey on his conduct. As usual he got his way
on "grounds of principle and British rights". *Bona-fide* British
shipping was not to be molested. This, however, was as much as
Maitland asked. While he agreed that means should be taken
to get rid of the "disgraceful traffic in human flesh and blood"
he considered it would be foolish for Britain to interfere with
the piracy that benefited her so much.

During the negotiations at Amiens in 1802, Bonaparte had
pierced this flaw in Britain's moral armour by proposing joint
action against the Barbary States. In 1815 the strength of
Abolitionist feeling in England compelled the Government to
get an international declaration against the slave trade. To allay
the charge of hypocrisy for being so concerned over *black*
slavery, Castlereagh decided next to offer a token of Britain's
sincerity. Lord Exmouth's fleet being still in the Mediterranean,
it was ordered to winter there.

Early the next summer (1816) the Admiral visited Algiers,
Tunis and Tripoli, ransoming slaves and, except in Algiers,
securing a promise to abolish Christian slavery. It was a fine
gesture and this should have completed it. Unfortunately, a

near-rupture at Algiers led to the massacre of 200 innocent coral fishers off Bona. Word of this reached London just as Exmouth anchored in Spithead. Hoots instead of cheers greeted his arrival in the capital. So quite against its original intention the Government was obliged to send him back with force enough "to teach the Dey a lesson".

The details of this famous expedition need not concern us. Suffice to say that on 27 August 1816, after the most careful preparations, Exmouth bearded the Algerian lion in his formidable lair, blew the corsair fleet out of the water, demolished the mole, bombarded the town, and then struggled out to sea again, his own fleet badly mauled. Fortunately the Dey, too, had had enough and agreed to abolish Christian slavery and release his slaves. But nothing was done or attempted about piracy. That continued. In no time the city and ships were rebuilt and the old profitable trade resumed. By the end of the year the fortifications were reported stronger than ever.

After this it was clear that Barbary piracy would never be extinguished unless some strong power established itself on the North African coast. There was thus every excuse for France's action in 1830 on moral and utilitarian grounds, though Britain would certainly not have accepted it had she not herself been engaged in domestic controversy. As it was, she extracted from the French Government a promise to withdraw as soon as its work was done. Britain was naturally alarmed at this rebirth of France's old ambition and obvious resolve to resume her place as an imperial power. Moreover, the years after 1830 coincided with commercial rivalry between the two powers and Russia in the Levant, and the development of Mediterranean steam navigation to a point where it seemed likely to halve the journey to the East. As French merchants and administrators were entrenched in Mehemet Ali's Egypt through which lay the short land bridge on the route to India, it was plain that France would have to be reckoned with again as Britain's chief rival for Mediterranean power.

For a third of a century after 1830 British foreign policy was dictated by Lord Palmerston who, like Canning, was ever suspicious of France and Russia and distrustful of congresses in which Britain was bound to find herself outvoted by the Eastern despotisms with their repressive interventionist notions. It is true that he himself was prepared to "intermeddle" (as he called it); but he did so from the vantage-point outside the European concert which Canning had won for England. Moreover his aim was always to preserve the peace and British interests by promoting timely concession. To foreign governments the liberal imperialism of this John Bull was often trying but to their peoples it held out a message of hope. This was especially true in the Mediterranean, where the forces of Liberalism and Nationalism were most eruptive, the conflict of power politics was coming to a head, and the influence of sea power could be most readily exerted.

In the Eastern Mediterranean Palmerston made use of British sea power based on Malta to restrain the ambitions of Russia and France in Constantinople and Cairo. He never sympathized with the spirit of nationality anywhere, and eastward of Greece his Liberal principles notoriously did not apply. But it was a different matter in the Western Mediterranean where Spain and Italy were in chronic Liberal revolt and Italy in particular a constant danger to European stability.

In Spain, the 'thirties were the era of the Carlist Wars, brutal, blood-thirsty civil wars in which, as in our own time, East and West intervened for power purposes behind an ideological mask. But the Eastern powers were farthest from the scene. From behind his wall of ships Palmerston was free to intermeddle as he pleased. He encouraged private Englishmen to volunteer, eased the purchase and distribution of ships and arms and, by the Quadruple Alliance of 1834, enlisted the support of France on behalf of the "Liberal" governments of Spain and Portugal. Where French and English fears and interests had competed violently, Palmerston managed to draw the two nations together to display a united front to the Eastern despotisms. This policy did nothing for Spain, the Constitutionalists who won being barely distinguishable from the Carlists they defeated. Spain remained a cypher in European affairs and to that extent perhaps served British interests. Nevertheless France was prevented from interfering in an area where she felt a special responsibility.

It was in Italy, however, that Palmerston's principles were

put to the fullest test. In Italy even more than in Greece British public opinion had to be reckoned with in deciding policy; for England and Italy had long been culturally and economically linked. Yet while Britain had traditionally close relations with Piedmont and Naples and big commercial dealings with Leghorn, these would hardly be affected whether Italy remained a congeries of tiny states or became a united nation. British interests would only be affected if the Vienna settlement were upset to the advantage of France—if France took advantage of Liberal and Nationalist sentiment to drive out Austria and dominate Italy herself.

This, unfortunately, appeared only too likely. France was not only Britain's natural enemy; she was to Austria in Italy very much what Russia was to Turkey in the Balkans. Palmerston succeeded in Italy where he failed in eastern Europe because he was able in the one case to rely on the dominating influence of sea power and the force of English Liberal sentiment. In the Balkans, however, the reach of sea power was all too limited and Liberal sentiment did not stretch so far. Where Italy was freed and united as a result of French aggression, Russia was driven back by European intervention on behalf of the Turk and the nations of eastern Europe were left in their dangerous servitude.

Palmerston was first confronted with the Italian problem in 1830, and his experience then determined his future attitude. Not only was Italy—this time central Italy—affected, France was too. In place of the restored Bourbon dynasty the July Revolution in Paris substituted the Citizen King, Louis Philippe. Owing his title to a popular movement, would he not be tempted like former revolutionaries to go to the succour of Italian Liberals and, by challenging Austria, plunge Europe into another series of revolutionary wars? Partly because of Palmerston's influence this did not happen. Nevertheless, Palmerston paid heed. Henceforward he saw in Italy one of the danger spots of Europe, and warned Metternich that Austria would never achieve stability except under forms of government in keeping with the spirit of the age.

In this spirit, on the eve of the next revolutionary year, 1848, he sent Lord Minto on a tour of Italian capitals to persuade

their rulers to grant reforms whilst there was time. The ide
was statesmanlike; one is reminded of the earlier Minto'
(Sir Gilbert Elliot's) similar efforts to unite the Italian
militarily. But the timing was bad. By 1847 conspiracy wa
already giving place to open revolt. The visit accordingl
partook more of an incitement of the people to rebel than a
inducement to their rulers to concede reform. It was accident
such as this that earned the conservative Palmerston hi
reputation as fomenter of revolution.

The revolutions of 1848 were an even greater danger to th
peace than those of 1830. Except for England and Russia al
Europe seemed affected. In general, Palmerston rejoiced at th
overthrow of his absolutist rivals; but in Italy he again watche
events with misgiving. Sicily led the way, in January 184
declaring for Bentinck's Constitution of 1812. A month later, i
Paris, the Second Republic was born, and in December Loui
Bonaparte, nephew of the great Napoleon, was elected i
President by popular vote. As he owed his elevation to his bein
Napoleon's heir, a career of foreign conquest seemed marke
out for him, above all in Italy where Napoleon's greates
triumphs had been won.

In face of this crisis Palmerston attained new statur
Begging and bullying he pressed moderation upon Vienna an
Paris. When Piedmont declared war on Austria, and Lombard
and Venice seemed lost to the Hapsburgs, he advised them t
accept the situation rather than expose Europe to war and them
selves to destruction. When the tide turned in their favour h
still counselled moderation, for he felt sure that Austria would b
stronger without the Italian encumbrance. To the astonishmen
of his fellow countrymen, he even welcomed the advent of th
new French President as a guarantee of order. Napoleon and h
worked together for a moderate settlement. That in the end
general war was avoided and the Vienna settlement restore
again owed much to Palmerston. It was hardly his fault tha
reaction set in afterwards with redoubled vigour.

It was not till the third crisis that Italy won her liberty. Th
creator of the new Italy was Count Cavour, Prime Minister c
the constitutional state of Piedmont. After the collapse of th
movement of 1848 Cavour was convinced that Italy would nev

e able to free herself from foreign domination without foreign
elp, which could only come from France. Bonaparte, now
Emperor as Napoleon III, was very ready to give it—up to a
oint—to please the Liberals and Bonapartists at home. But
omplete Italian unification would mean putting an end to the
Papal States, and that would offend Catholic sentiment. The
nost he contemplated, therefore, was a loose confederation of
tates under the presidency of the Pope. Nevertheless the part
e played was essential. By beating Austria in battle he en-
ouraged Italians to throw in their lot with Cavour's Piedmont
under King Victor Emmanuel. On the other hand the hasty truce
t Villafranca in July 1859 left Austria in possession of Venice
nd in a position to reassert her authority over the peninsula.
Such an Italy would have been a battleground. It was not a
olution to satisfy either Cavour or Palmerston. Italians generally
vere disgusted, moreover, when the Emperor took Nice and
Savoy as the price of his assistance. Palmerston's achievement
ay in resolving this humiliating stalemate to produce a unified
talian kingdom.

Palmerston came into office as Premier almost as the
Franco-Austrian War began in the summer of 1859. Lord John
Russell was his Foreign Secretary, and in this cause the two old
ivals worked enthusiastically together. Distrusting Napoleon's
ntentions, they took pains to justify the popular movement in
entral Italy for union with Piedmont by reference to Britain's
wn Glorious Revolution of 1688. They used the same doctrine
f popular self-determination to deny the right of either France
r Austria to interfere in favour of a confederation. When
Garibaldi the "filibuster" ('What was William of Orange but a
ilibuster?') conquered Sicily with his famous Thousand in
May 1860, they discountenanced Napoleon's proposal of joint
leet action to prevent his passing over to the mainland.
Consequently, when King Victor Emmanuel, having occupied
he Papal States, met Garibaldi in Naples in November 1860
he Kingdom of Italy became a reality. To foreign protests at
uch methods Russell retorted with his celebrated dispatch of
27 October 1860, affirming the people the best judge of their
wn affairs. That dispatch, Cavour said, was worth more than
100,000 men.

I

Britain's part in Italian liberation has no doubt been exaggerated by English historians. It was certainly just as much dictated by self-interest as Napoleon's. The difference was that at that time the interests of Britain as a Mediterranean power coincided with helping the Italians to find a peaceful and permanent solution of their problems. Palmerston was no advocate of nationality, but he did want a solution that would not profit France or weaken England. He was able to achieve this because Liberals at home backed him up, and nothing could be done in the Italian peninsula without the tacit consent of the British Navy.

It is important to add that while Italian unification marked a wide-scale abandonment of the Vienna settlement in detail, it nonetheless sustained it in principle so far as Britain was concerned. Austria was not unduly weakened in central Europe. A united Italy proved a tougher obstacle to French trans-Alpine adventures than Austria could have been. Italy's sense of obligation and the vulnerability of her coasts to naval action enhanced Britain's Mediterranean position; and the ties between the two countries were further strengthened by Britain's ability to supply the coal and iron that Italy needed.

Italy's liberation was effected in a nervous international atmosphere. The coming of the screw-propelled iron-clad warship had led to a naval race with France; while the growing traffic on the Mediterranean route to the East distracted attention from Russia, defeated in the Crimea, and directed it instead to French progress in Egypt and Syria. The year of Napoleon's Italian campaign saw the first sod turned in de Lessep's canal at Suez and Palmerston's conversion to the idea of a steam navy. Notwithstanding the protests of Gladstone as Chancellor of the Exchequer, it was found advisable to double the garrisons at Gibraltar and Malta and undertake costly works at the latter to turn it into a first-class naval base. It was in this state of tension between military preparation and fiscal economy that Palmerston took advantage of a revolution in Athens to cede the Ionian Islands to Greece.

The hope of a sufficiently strong and Liberal Greek State emerging as a barrier against Russia had been disappointed. The Ionian Protectorate had been equally disappointing and somewhat embarrassing. Corfu had never seemed worth developing as a naval base, and now what money there was had to be put into Malta. What better solution, then, than to capitalize on the enthusiasm aroused by Russell's Italian policy to cede the islands to Greece and produce a similarly grateful state at the foot of that peninsula? So in 1863 the islands were handed over as a kind of dowry to a king of England's choice, known to history as King George of Greece. This generous gesture was unhappily soiled in the execution. In giving up Corfu, Britain was more than ever determined that it should never again fall into the possession of France or Russia. So the fortifications were demolished and the islands neutralized. The pique of the Greeks at this more than quenched any sense of gratitude.

The end of the era of Palmerston coincided with the exhaustion of Nationalist and Liberal agitation in western and central Europe, and ushered in for England a period of deceptive quiet. The naval race with France was easily won. Britain had coal and iron at her door and no other nation could compare with her as yet in industrial skill. The strategic vantage points secured in the wars with France were now turned into coaling stations studding the world's sea routes. At home, with better times, a sense of complacency appeared, punctuated by a mild reform bill. Overseas, the advantages of free trade, finally accepted about 1860, seemed amply demonstrated by expanding commerce, shipping and investment. The mid-Victorian felt at liberty to luxuriate awhile among Gladstonian abstractions.

In this state of mind the full meaning of events on the Continent was not at first perceived. In 1866 Austria was driven out of Germany and Venice and urged towards the Balkans. In 1870 Napoleon's Empire was overwhelmed and the German Empire proclaimed at Versailles; Italian unity was completed by the entry into Rome; and Russia, repudiating the penalties imposed on her in 1856, resumed her progress towards the Bosphorus. As the Suez Canal had just been opened and was already monopolized by British shipping, the Eastern Question was raised in a new and acute form. Of the European equilibrium bequeathed by Pitt and Castlereagh little was left except the British Mediterranean fleet. There reappeared, instead, a bloc of Eastern despotisms dominated now less by ungainly Russia than by the efficient Bismarkian state.

Britain's tardy response to these developments was the new Imperial note struck by Disraeli. Tory democracy at home was to be associated with world attitudes abroad. Where Canning had called in America, Disraeli summoned Asia to redress the balance in Europe. He made the inspired purchase of the Suez Canal shares and Queen Victoria became Empress of India. To consolidate the white colonies plans of Imperial Federation were mooted. It was no new thing. Britain had defied France for centuries, had brought Napoleon down, by confronting the Continent with the resources of the world overseas. But at this moment it was a striking and even dangerous gesture Britain could afford no less; but that she could afford so much was in itself a challenge to the rest of Europe. The interest in India increased friction with Russia, concern for Egypt that with France. The Mediterranean becoming the commercial highway of the Empire, Suez appeared more important than the Dardanelles.

In the next Balkan crisis, Disraeli felt impelled to lend British support once more to the Turk, and shipped Indian troops ostentatiously through Suez to Malta to reinforce his demand for a general conference on Balkan affairs. He acquired the island of Cyprus as a reward for past and trust for future services to the Porte. All this was much. But it was ominous that the Congress which in 1878 put new bounds to Russia's advance met at Berlin under the presidency of Bismarck. Equally ominous was Disraeli's need, in securing Cyprus, to bribe France with the promise of Tunis. For France was by now maturing the Imperial designs founded at Algiers half a century before.

So far, apart from Algiers, Britain had succeeded in preserving North Africa from European political intrusion, but the pressure could not be resisted indefinitely. At first the weakness of Spain and the Italian states made France the only power to be reckoned with, and her progress had been slow. Nevertheless she soon came into contact with the neighbouring regency of Tunis and the empire of Morocco. Palmerston's reaction is well illustrated in the case of Morocco.

Morocco had always been a live strategic area, and it had long been Britain's aim to monopolize its trade and maritime goodwill. Palmerston was content to neutralize it politically, while leaving it open to commercial penetration. By impressing on the Emperor his dependence on Britain, he hoped to persuade him to give way on minor points of friction with foreign powers so as to ensure Britain's support on major ones. In this policy Palmerston was ably supported by his consular agents, the Drummond Hays, father and son, who dominated Moroccan politics throughout the middle quarters of the century. Their task was never easy; for although the Emperor had renounced privateering as a state activity, he had difficulty restraining the piratical Rif tribesmen of his north-east coast, who were continually bringing down the anger of the powers on their suzerain's head. The worst crises, those of 1836 and 1844, concerned France, and led to the visit of French naval squadrons to Moroccan ports and even a land offensive. Nevertheless, from these and other predicaments John Drummond Hay, by persuading the Emperor to yield on inessentials, rescued his empire intact.

Palmerston had been equally sensitive to any encroachment on Tunis. It was one of his reasons for opposing Mehemet Ali. Anxious to be on good terms with Palmerston who, he knew, did not trust him, Napoleon III restrained the popular clamour for further North African advance. But this merely left the way open for the new Kingdom of Italy which now entered its claim for Mediterranean dominion. Italians had long been settled in Tunis as traders, and after 1860 they began to come in in greater numbers. Italy's difficulty lay in finding, not colonists, but capital, and at first France and Britain monopolized the commercial concessions. The Bey getting into debt to them, in 1869 they stepped in, associating Italy with them, to secure their interest on the Tunisian revenues. When Britain dropped out ten years later, Italy purchased her railway concessions. But sensing the danger, France, supported by Disraeli's promise and Bismarck's prompting, decided on anticipatory action, and a border foray gave her the excuse to establish a protectorate in 1881.

The seizure of Tunis gave much provocation. The Eastern Question was intensified. Britain's route to the East, growing daily in importance, lost its frontier aspect; and it was only a lucky accident that gave her a foothold in Egypt the following year. The two empires seemed fated to renew their centuries-old rivalry in a contest to which the Mediterranean would be the key. More sinister still was the hardening of the European states system into opposing camps. Furious at being outwitted, Italy clamoured for admission to Bismarck's central *bloc*; the Triple Alliance of 1882 registered her success and completed France's isolation.

Having joined issue in the colonial field, France and Britain did not find themselves alone. Political consolidation and the pressure of industrialism made other powers increasingly anxious for access to oversea markets. Germany joined in the race, and Africa was shared out till only Morocco, Tripoli, Abyssinia and Liberia were unappropriated. In Europe itself a similar movement was seen. On the grim Balkan racial conflicts was now imposed Austro-Russian rivalry for economic privilege, thus adding another chapter to the Eastern Question. Other countries besides Britain were realizing the need to be "great" if their peoples were not to be condemned to permanently low standards of living. Their gathering resentment, unhappily, was chiefly directed at her.

Under the spell of Disraeli Britain had begun to look outwards to India and the self-governing colonies that had grown up almost unnoticed in an age of imperial nonchalance. Jolted suddenly, she now turned inwards to re-examine her position in Europe and the strength of her Navy. In 1884 there was a scare of war over her status in Egypt, which the French could not forgive. France this time had German backing, and it was noted that their combined navies outnumbered Britain's in capital ships. As the French were gradually shifting the balance of their naval strength from Brest and Cherbourg to Toulon, the security of the Mediterranean route came directly into question.

It was not clear whether the French move was aimed more

at Italy or at Britain. At any rate the two powers came together in an alliance arranged by Lord Salisbury in 1887 to last for five years. They agreed to oppose further French expansion in North Africa and guarantee the *status quo* throughout the Mediterranean. To this Mediterranean Agreement, as it was called, Austria-Hungary also shortly adhered. Bismarck sympathized with the arrangements because he wanted, like Salisbury, to keep the "two unstable elements", France and Russia, separate. The effect, however, was quite the contrary. Feeling their isolation, France and Russia made tentative approaches until in 1894 they confronted the world with the Dual Alliance.

Britain was consequently faced with the combination she dreaded most. In face of it, the naval entanglement with Italy was a dubious asset. In 1889 the "Two-Power Standard" had been asserted, implying a marginal superiority over the two next strongest powers. As these were Russia and France, now allied and building fast, the naval building programme was again feverishly speeded up in 1895. How right the decision was seemed fully borne out the following year, when the Kaiser's message to President Kruger of the Transvaal after the Jameson Raid exposed Britain's isolation. The Mediterranean Agreements were not renewed; but the problem remained how best to dispose the Mediterranean fleet so as to dominate Toulon and at the same time check any Russian irruption through the Dardanelles. There seemed no way of attaining both objects without running a risk of piecemeal defeat. So grave was the peril that naval experts seriously considered abandoning the Mediterranean altogether and 'sealing it at both ends'.

Broadly speaking, it was the traditional answer that was adopted. Little heed was taken of the new French North African bases, as France was thought to be weakened the more she dispersed her strength. While the Mediterranean fleet, Britain's most powerful, was divided between Gibraltar and Malta, the Channel fleet was given Gibraltar as its rendezvous. A small Levant squadron was thrown off to deceive the Russians. In the event of hostilities with France the Mediterranean fleet was to assemble at Malta, withdraw to Gibraltar, and thence, in company with the Channel fleet assume the offensive in the Mediterranean.

To meet the needs of this increased activity and the revolutionary changes which now took place in warship size and design, Britain's two bases had also to be transformed. In 1893 work was begun to convert Gibraltar for the first time into a first-class naval base, complete with docks, efficient coaling yards, and breakwater defences against torpedo attack. The Malta yards had already been enlarged twice within a period of twenty years. In 1899 it was proposed to extend them further and add a torpedo-proof breakwater. Under stress, Britain, far from evacuating the Mediterranean, was showing her resolve to remain the greatest Mediterranean power.

The nineteenth century ended, therefore, as it had begun, with Britain still supreme at sea and doggedly ensconced in her Mediterranean bases. If such a thing were possible, the value of sea power to her had actually increased during the century, and with it the importance of the Mediterranean as route and pincer. Correspondingly, however, it was becoming abundantly clear that her imperial status was no longer privileged, her control of the world's strategic axis no longer to be taken for granted. The harsh fact was that the armed camps of the Triple and Dual Alliances were only divided on European issues. On world issues, those with which Britain's fate was tied, they were practically united in their opposition to her. Against Russia and France she might have expected to hold her own; but as the twentieth century dawned the fact could not be blinked that a more serious rival than either or both of them had arisen.

CHAPTER VIII

THE GERMAN WARS, 1900-45

GERMANY'S decision in 1897 to build a first-class navy was not thought unreasonable at the time. Indeed, for several years Britain took little notice of the new development, but continued to watch France and Russia. Joseph Chamberlain even sought a defensive alliance with Germany as a way out of Britain's isolation. Nevertheless, the steadily growing power of the German Navy was to exert a controlling influence on British policy right down to the outbreak of war in 1914. Attention was suddenly seen to be fixed on Kiel and the North Sea instead of the Mediterranean.

The alliance with Japan in 1902 was, perhaps, Britain's first confession of her inability to stand alone. Besides checking Russia, it eased the naval pressure in home waters. The next move, intended as a mere clearing of the air, gave birth un-wittingly to a diplomatic revolution. This was the agreement with France in 1904 on outstanding oversea questions. France had by this time expanded over most of northern and western Africa and regarded herself as very nearly a "satisfied" power. Excluded from the upper Nile she set her heart on compensation in Morocco to round off her African Empire. With this in view she made a secret agreement with Italy in 1900 while Britain was absorbed in the Boer War. Hurt that her understanding with Britain had brought her so far such little profit, Italy agreed to surrender to France her claims in Morocco in return for a free hand in Tripoli. The effect on Britain was to increase her sense of isolation and encourage her to extend the policy of regional agreements already tried out in the Mediterranean and the Far East. This was the atmosphere in which Delcassé made the historic approach to Lord Lansdowne which brought the Dual Entente into being.

The crucial issue was the future of Morocco. British interests there were older and more substantial than French. At the

moment, however, Britain was more concerned over Egypt
France was consequently able to use her own strong claims i
that country as an effective bargaining counter. The problem
was complicated by the fact that Spain and Germany were als
interested in Morocco. Spain still held Ceuta and some smal
Rif outposts and, in spite of a century of internal weakness an
the disastrous American war, her sense of mission had no
diminished. A recent campaign in the British Press asserting th
vulnerability of Gibraltar from the land side had been taken u
vigorously by patriotic Spanish voices. Accordingly, no Britis
Government could consider a Moroccan settlement that di
not have Spanish approval or that permitted the fortification o
the African shore of the Straits. As for Germany, her economi
interests were by now second only to those of Britain. Partl
for that reason she was the one power whom Delcassé wa
determined to exclude. But Lansdowne wisely insisted on a
"open door" and on Germany's equality of status, as due bot
to her existing treaty rights and her stature as a Great Power.

The Anglo-French Convention of 8 April 1904 sought t
resolve these difficulties. Egypt and Morocco were recognized
as, respectively, British and French preserves, though the ope
door was to be maintained. The political *status quo*, it was agreed
should also be kept; but here came the rub. In secret article
Britain and France planned the protectorates which were to b
set up in the event of this policy breaking down. For example
Morocco was to be shared by France and Spain, the coas
opposite Gibraltar becoming a Spanish sphere of influence on
condition it should not be fortified. If Spanish interests were
thus taken into account, those of Germany were, after all,
implicitly excluded. This was serious enough. Graver still wa
the fact that Britain's concern for Egypt had tied her to France'
apron strings in Morocco. For while, as was desired, the Convention removed Egypt from the field of international controversy, it had no such effect on Morocco. France was free to se
the pace and, so long as she kept to the letter of this doubtfu
transaction, Britain was bound to follow. This was the price
Britain had to pay for her security in Egypt and the sharing o
her Mediterranean responsibilities.

The truth soon dawned on Germany that she had been left

out of a colonial partition agreement in which she felt legally
and morally entitled to share. Her population rising rapidly,
her industry expanding, and with an enormous military and
naval expenditure, she felt with growing urgency the pressure
on world markets. No government could survive which failed
to stake a German claim to every remaining oversea asset. It
is not surprising, perhaps, that in its haste the Kaiser's Government blundered and provoked the very thing it wanted to avoid.
Seeing France pushing on with plans for Moroccan "reform",
it decided to affirm Germany's rights under the 1880 international treaty on Morocco. In the spring of 1905 the Kaiser
was induced to land from his yacht at Tangier and give
Germany's assurance of Moroccan independence and the
maintenance of the open door. His Government followed this up
by demanding a conference of the signatories of the 1880 treaty.

Delcassé's policy had thus been challenged from a formidable
quarter. If France accepted the challenge war must result. What
would Britain do? The reckoning had not been long in coming.
Lord Lansdowne's attitude was rather undecided. While firm
enough in his determination to prevent Germany acquiring
compensation in the shape of Atlantic bases at Agadir or
Mogador, he tried not to commit Britain too rashly in a
French quarrel. Delcassé was not to be fobbed off, however. He
interpreted Lansdowne's offer of a degree of co-operation in
"any contingencies" as the promise of military assistance.

Luckily, the French Government, though convinced of
Britain's support, was still too nervous to meet Germany's
challenge. Delcassé fell, and the German plan of a conference
was accepted, to be held at Algéciras the following year. There
Germany to her astonishment found herself unsupported by the
very powers whose interests she claimed to be defending. While
the principle of the open door and respect for treaties was
re-affirmed, it was at the price of consolidating the Entente
Cordiale, now backed by Russia and Italy, Germany's supposed
allies.

This first Moroccan crisis had been as much for Britain as
for France a test of the new power system. Originating in the
need to secure Egypt and Suez, the Entente now implied acceptance of the twentieth-century principle that the control of the

Mediterranean was to be shared with France. The principle soon received practical endorsement. When in 1904 Sir John Fisher became First Sea Lord he reversed the naval distribution accepted in the 'nineties, withdrawing the Mediterranean fleet from Malta to Gibraltar so that, as the Atlantic fleet, it could act with the Channel fleet against Germany. This was a public measure. It was supported in 1906 by military and naval talks with France which, though authorized by Lansdowne's successor, Grey, and the Prime Minister, Campbell-Bannerman, were unknown to the Cabinet as a whole. Insist as Grey might that Britain retained her freedom of action, the Government and through it the nation was, in fact, morally committed to the obligations of an alliance. The conclusion in 1907 of a convention with France's partner, Russia, defining spheres of influence from Persia to Tibet, completed Britain's revised security system.

Germany, meanwhile, had been taking Britain's place as defender of the Porte. In 1908 her ally, Austria-Hungary, annexed the provinces of Bosnia and Herzogovina, thereby tearing up a treaty, affronting Balkan nationalism and challenging Russia who, since her defeat by Japan, had been forced once again to seek her warm-water outlet by way of European Turkey. Grey lodged his protest, but did not deny Russia's right in compensation to re-open the Straits, provided it were done by international agreement. So far had the pendulum swung. In the event, the Bosnian crisis, after threatening war, was decided by the humiliation of Russia, and with her, by implication, the other Entente powers.

Meanwhile, the naval competition was further embittering Anglo-German relations. Where Germany emphasized her right to become a world power through the medium of a navy, Britain insisted on the need of naval supremacy to maintain her position as a world power. In growing tension arising from the crippling armaments expenditure the Moroccan settlement broke down. Still anxious lest Germany should acquire an Atlantic base Grey in 1907 agreed to an exchange of notes between the Entente and Spain promising consultation in case of any threat to the *status quo* in the Mediterranean or the eastern Atlantic. About the same time French troops occupied

certain Moroccan towns. A year later Grey supported France
diplomatically in a trivial dispute with Germany at Casablanca.
In February 1909 France and Germany made a last attempt at
collaboration. But it did not prove feasible; so when, in May
1911, a native rising led the French to occupy the capital, and
Spain took possession of two towns in her assigned zone,
Germany declared the Algeçiras Treaty at an end. The gunboat
Panther was sent to Agadir to protect German commercial
interests and establish a claim to compensation when the
imminent partition should take place.

In the crisis that this precipitated, Grey recognized that all
three powers had "stepped outside the Algeçiras Act". His
attitude was as ambiguous as Lansdowne's had been. On the
one hand he felt bound to give France the utmost support short
of war. On the other hand he admitted Germany's right to some
compensation. If, however, this were exacted on either coast of
Morocco or otherwise threatened a vital British interest he was
ready to fight. On the earlier occasion it had been Germany
insisting on her "rights"; this time it was Britain who would not
brook "humiliation". The fleet was prepared for action in case
the Germans should attempt a *coup*. The settlement arrived at
in November 1911, by which France received a free hand in
Morocco in return for cessions to Germany in the Congo had
thus the appearance of having been come to under the muzzle of
British naval guns. While Britain joined with France to uphold
the Mediterranean equilibrium and helped her complete her
African Empire, Germany again felt thwarted because of her
lack of sufficient power at sea. Her helplessness the same year
when Italy seized Tripoli from her ally, Turkey, pointed the
same lesson.

The failure of the Liberals to follow up the naval initiative
seized by Fisher put new heart into German naval building.
Competition with Britain was already proceeding at a financially
ruinous pace when, stung by these events, Germany in 1912
introduced a yet more aggressive Naval Law. The same crisis
had brought Mr. Winston Churchill to the Admiralty. His
initial response to the Naval Law was the ingenious offer of
a "naval holiday". When this was rejected he produced a
counter-balancing British programme and a further redistribu-

tion of the fleet. The Malta squadron was to take the place of th
Atlantic squadron at Gibraltar; the Atlantic squadron was to b
moved into home waters.

This "abandonment of the Mediterranean" was certain!
not intended to be absolute; a cruiser squadron was to be kep
at Malta and strengthened by battleships as soon as they becam
available. Nevertheless the concurrent French decision to ma
their navy in the Mediterranean did mean—though Mr. Churchi
himself denied it in principle—that the two nations were nov
in effect, acting as one. While Britain's interest in Egypt an
the extent of Austrian naval building led her to assume a mor
direct responsibility for the Eastern Mediterranean and th
Adriatic, France, being militarily dependent on her Africa
garrisons, was assigned the western basin and the task of cover
ing the Italian fleet. All naval facilities were to be share
Malta might become, in effect, a French naval base.

Such was the naval situation in the Mediterranean when, i
August 1914, a match struck in the Balkans exploded the entir
European powder magazine. To this fatality events in the Wester
Mediterranean had contributed more, probably, than even
anywhere else. That this was so was due on the one hand to th
universal recognition of its strategic importance, on the othe
to the fact that Britain's nineteenth-century imperial system wa
in process of giving place to another based on co-operation wit
France.

The first German War was fought on similar lines to th
great wars with France. The differences were mainly superficia
British armies played a more important part on land than eve
before. Instead, moreover, of the accustomed clash of battl
fleets in Atlantic and Mediterranean, there was the stalemate i
the North Sea. Yet the only essential difference was in th
location of the enemy and in his fighting quality. Germany, lik
France of old, was as far as possible encircled, first by alliance
with Russia, Italy and the Balkan powers, then by the vas
co-ordinated pressure of sea blockade, exerted this time not b
Britain alone but by Britain and France and other strong nava
powers. The German High Seas Fleet was kept bottled up in it
corner of the North Sea more securely than it had ever bee

possible to contain the scattered squadrons of France. From first to last the active role of the German Navy was confined to commerce destruction.

Until the portentous advent of the submarine, the only real weakness in the Allied encircling system—apart, that is, from the direct threat to France and the Channel ports by land—was the spear of German influence down the Danube and across the Dardanelles to the Persian Gulf or Egypt. This was the weakness that Napoleon had divined. It not only opened a way to divide the Allies strategically and close the Suez route; it offered Germany access to Balkan and Ukranian corn and a prospect of Persian oil which the Allies badly needed themselves. For these reasons, Central and Allied powers alike, after the failure of the initial attempt at a knock-out blow in the west, gave increasing attention to the south-east. Neither, however, concentrated adequately on that region.

In August 1914 Mediterranean strategy was complicated by the uncertain attitude of Italy, whose ties with the Central Powers though weakened politically were strong economically, and whose policy was known to be opportunist. To begin with, therefore, the original naval plan had to be followed. A French naval commander-in-chief was appointed and given Malta as a forward base. The French Navy covered the transport routes from Algiers and Tunis and accepted responsibility for the Italian fleet. The British fleet covered the Adriatic, the Canal and the Eastern Mediterranean generally. There was curiously little anxiety over what Turkey should do, perhaps because she had no fleet or because Britain was too concerned for the safety of her own commerce on the high seas. The German battle-cruiser *Goeben* and the cruiser *Breslau*, which had been lying at Messina, were consequently able to bombard Bona and Philippeville, outwit the Malta squadron and escape into the Dardanelles. Fictitiously bought by the Turk, they entered the Black Sea and gave provocation which helped to bring Turkey into the war three months later on the German side. The Austrian fleet being shut in the Adriatic, the Western Mediterranean was now safe enough. But at the eastern end Russia was cut off from her allies and the Suez Canal vulnerable from the land side.

The close of the year bringing stalemate on the main fronts both sides the next year sought a way out of the impasse by pressure on south-eastern Europe. The Dardanelles campaign and the landing at Salonika which followed it, were attempts by the Allies to exploit Mediterranean control against Germany's *Mittel-Europa*, after the fashion of Marlborough's Toulon design or the economic paralysis of the Continental blockade. If France had not been so absorbed with the Western Front the Dardanelles expedition, being prosecuted with vigour, must have put Turkey out of the war. The Middle East would thus have been cleared, succour brought to Russia, and an inviting passage opened through to Vienna by way of the Hapsburg national minorities. Instead, that spring the Germans thrust the Russians back out of Poland and the following autumn harried the broken Serbian Army over the Albanian mountains to Durazzo, whence it was taken off by the Allied fleet and carried to Salonika. Bulgaria declaring for the Central Powers in November 1915, the Allies were divided west from east by a Berlin-Bagdad bloc and the collapse of Russia was only a question of time. So far-reaching were the consequences of failure to develop the traditional vigorous Mediterranean offensive.

By this time, moreover, Germany was beginning to employ the instrument with which she hoped to turn against the Allies the whole system of blockade. The submarine campaign was the twentieth-century version of the Guerre de Course, but infinitely more deadly. The Mediterranean's narrow channels were especially suited to submarine operations. The exploits of German and British commanders in the Dardanelles itself are sufficiently well known. Against transports and supply ships feeding Gallipoli and Salonika the Germans inflicted heavy losses and enforced circuitous, time-consuming journeys. Fortunately, the full fury of U-boat warfare could not be unleashed except at the price of bringing the United States in on the Allied side.

After the evacuation of Gallipoli in December 1915 two southern fronts were left. In May 1915 Italy, stimulated by the Gallipoli landings and the rich promises held out to her by the secret Treaty of London, declared war on Austria-Hungary

Ier armies pushed unsuccessfully across the Isonzo towards he coveted ports of Pola and Trieste. To pass the Alps from the outhern side would have been difficult indeed; but victory on he Isonzo would have assured command of the Adriatic and pened a route into the heart of the Hapsburg lands. It was not a threat that the Austrians could ignore. The Salonika front, on he other hand, had been opened defensively. At first it had been loped to assist the Serbs. Later, Corfu having been seized by he French and King Constantine deposed for his German ympathies, the lines at Salonika became a bastion guarding he Greek peninsula. Thus once again the Mediterranean peninsulas were denied to Britain's enemy. Although the heavy rontal assaults in the west precluded the launching of major ttacks from the south, the southern fronts were nevertheless irmly maintained. Haig's attack at Cambrai in November 1917 was undertaken, and five British divisions lent, to help stem the hrust on the Piave after the rout of Caporetto on the upper Isonzo.

The great submarine offensive was begun in February 1917. In the Mediterranean it exacted its heaviest toll, and continued here little abated until the summer of 1918. Cattaro, in lower Dalmatia and scene of Hoste's exploit, was the principal U-boat base. Vessels were brought in sections to the assembly-base at Pola at the foot of the Istrian peninsula and thence run down he channels behind the Dalmatian islands. In three weeks luring August 1916 a single commander had sunk fifty Allied steamers. By 1917 there were more than twenty operating from Cattaro. With a quarter of a million troops locked up in Egypt alone, Salonika a constant drain, Italy in stark need of munitions and Welsh coal, France chained to North Africa, and the busy Suez traffic to be kept moving, it is small wonder that the U-boat peril taxed Allied ingenuity. Various expedients were tried to cope with it. A net was drawn across the Straits of Otranto by a drifter flotilla, and the Mediterranean divided into patrol zones; but not even the gradual readoption of convoys in the summer of 1917 (under British direction from Malta), sufficed to remove the menace.

When the Germans made their final effort in the west in March 1918, they supported it by an intensified U-boat offensive

K

throughout the Mediterranean. Reinforcements hastily trans
ferred from Egypt and Palestine were an easy target. Thoug
the Allied patrols in the Straits of Gibraltar met with som
success, those in the Straits of Otranto proved quite ineffective
It was not until June that the expansion and systematization c
convoys reduced Mediterranean sinkings to less than a hundre
thousand tons a month. This, indeed, registered a great an
decisive, if long-delayed victory, second in importance only t
that in home waters which let in the Americans.

In the autumn of 1918 the army of Salonika provided som
self-justification by advancing to put Bulgaria and, as a con
sequence, Turkey, out of the war, and the Italians opened thei
final offensive across the Piave which brought them to triumpl
at Vittorio Veneto. The German Army, still intact but presse
back breathlessly on to its own frontiers, suddenly saw a broa
road of invasion opening in its rear. That this was a "stab in th
back" there can be no doubt, whatever the merit of th
argument of civil discontent.

To the end when it came on 11 November 1918 the effor
in the Mediterranean contributed no small part. It more tha
justified the revolution in British strategy which the Entent
with France implied. The Battle of the Mediterranean was wo
by the united efforts of the navies and merchant fleets of Britai
and France and their allies in a "vast composite exertion". I
seems certain, however, that the controlling strategists on bot
sides undervalued the possibilities inherent in the Mediterranea
flank. The proof would seem to lie in their attitude towards it i
the years of anxious peace and in the second great trial o
strength that lay ahead.

Looking back after another great war with Germany it i
only natural to see the years between as merely a period of truce
This is a correct view provided it is not allowed to obscure th
realities upon which British policy was based. The challenge o
German economic and military power between 1900 and 191
severely tested Britain's complex mercantile structure, a fabri
already strained by the growth of new industrial economies lik
those of the United States and Japan. After 1918, therefore
idealism and interest united to broaden still further the founda

tions of Britain's security system. Where in 1904-5 she had instinctively joined forces with her late enemy France, now in 1919 she earnestly, though of course not without reservations, sought her well-being in the collective security offered by the League of Nations.

It was in this frame of mind that British statesmen gave their attention to the problem of arranging the peace settlement. If the underlying principles of the Vienna Settlement had been security against the recent "aggressor" and the balance of power, so, properly speaking, were those of Versailles. But whereas security had then been sought in the principle of dynastic legitimacy and the erection of buffer states, this time it tended to be sought in victimizing the aggressor, in a comprehensive concert of all the powers, and in the moral sinews of the ideal of national self-determination. Of these new principles the first two implied provision for peaceful readjustment, but the third, unhappily, made such "revision" unlikely; for "self-determination" must be stopped at some point or there will be no security. Unhappily also, national idealism, having been so long frustrated over much of eastern and south-eastern Europe, had by this time become pathological and insisted on fulfilment in defiance of economic reality. As if these contradictions were not enough, moreover, the victor peoples were also burdened by promises given in the heat of the struggle. Those made to Italy, Russia, Greece, the Arabs and the Jews were all reflected in the Mediterranean scene.

The Mediterranean settlement embodied these contradictions. With the break-up of the Hapsburg Empire Balkan "liberation" was achieved, "Italia Irredenta" redeemed, but only at the price of economic impoverishment, a dangerous emphasis on the rights rather than the duties of minorities, and a vested opposition to further revision. On the surface Britain might have felt confirmed in her adoption of collective security. Constantinople, promised to Russia as a friend in 1915, was denied her as an enemy and left, after all, to the Turk; while Britain got some practical advantage from the "demilitarization" of the Straits which, if occasion again arose, the Navy would be in a position to force as it had never hitherto been able to do. The liberation of Asiatic Turkey might have seemed even more advantageous. With the Canal secured by treaty with Egypt in 1922, mandates in Iraq and Palestine and friendly relations with the whole Arab bloc, with France established in Syria and a friendly Italy in Libya, the imperial lifeline to India and Australasia and the access to oil and rubber might have appeared safer than ever before.

But how much of this imposing edifice was sound? In practice Arab nationalism, especially in Egypt, felt itself cheated. Racial or religious ties linked India to Morocco, covering the Mediterranean-Red Sea route and nearly all non-dollar oil. The entire area simmered with nationalist and economic discontent. For similar reasons the Balkan equilibrium was most uncertain, while at the western end of the Mediterranean Spain was maturing expansionist plans in Morocco. It was upon this delicate balance between the new order sponsored by the League and the vast underground opposition to it, the balance upon which Britain's imperial security now rested, that Italy petulantly brought her weight to bear. Before her pressure the new international order slowly crumbled.

Italy is a poor country but a populous one, with a proud past and natural ambitions which the established great powers have been loath to recognize. Like Japan, Italy must either be "great" or submit to a standard of welfare for her people inferior to their reasonable expectations. The contrast with Britain herself was all too striking in Italian eyes. When a great empire created by economic and military exertion, attempts to secure itself against dissolution on a basis of justice and international solidarity, it must needs face some searching tests. Italy's Mussolini, coming to power in 1922, saw his opportunity in this fact.

By the Treaty of London (1915) Italy had been promised more than the Allies had been able to perform. Though the dangerous Trentino wedge was pushed back to give her the line of the Brenner, she was left elsewhere a dissatisfied and therefore "revisionist" power. As British opinion felt guilty over her treatment, it was her case more than that of a defeated power like Germany, that became the test of the League's capacity to effect peaceful revision.

Italy was to begin with small territorial readjustments in

Africa or along the Adriatic coast, and follow this up by economic
penetration of the Balkans or the upper reaches of the Nile.
Behind this drive, however, lay not the new notion of "self-
determination", which would give her at best a claim on French
Tunisia, but the more primitive imperial drives associated
historically with Rome and the mediaeval republics, and
economically with the idea of living-space. Italy was the
prisoner of the Mediterranean, Mussolini once said. Unhappily
for her she is likely to remain so, as long as power approximates
to industrial and strategic strength. Englishmen, nevertheless,
could not but feel the force of Italy's claim. At the same time
it was clear that any revision in her favour would reopen claims
for revision elsewhere and cut across the principle of self-
determination. Such was the dilemma on which Britain was
impaled by the ambitions of Mussolini.

Until as late as 1935, in spite of spasmodic outbursts from
the Duce, Britons and Italians continued to accept their traditional friendship as axiomatic. The chief difference was over
Tangier where Italy was concerned because seventy per cent of
her trade passes through the Straits of Gibraltar. After an
injudicious rebuff in 1923, she was admitted in 1928 to the
International Control of the city. Britain had also been disturbed by Italian propaganda among the Moslem peoples and
by the social rift in Malta encouraged by Italian cultural aspirations. But differences such as these could occur among friends,
and Italy's quarrel seemed to lie chiefly with France from whom
she was severed by naval and commercial rivalry and North
African ambitions. Both nations, however, were conscious of their
weaknesses. Italy remembered her 5,000 miles of defenceless
coastline and big oceanic trade, France her dependence on
North Africa. Left to themselves they would hardly have come
to blows.

It was the Abyssinian crisis of 1935-6 that first impressed
Britain with the dangers inherent in Italian pretensions.
Opposition by Britain on anti-imperialist grounds to this
colonial venture could only have a hollow sound. As mouthpiece and naval instrument of the League of Nations, moreover,
much was expected of Britain both at home and abroad and
equally on grounds of idealism and interest. The British Govern-

ment took the lead in marshalling the nations in imposing "sanctions" as the Covenant of the League decreed. Equally on grounds of idealism and interest it was determined not to be led into war on this account. Germany had rearmed. The Anglo-German Naval Treaty had just been signed. France would not agree to any step which would alienate Italy further in face of the threat on the Rhine. League and security would both be shattered if the two dictators were driven together.

Consequently, while the Mediterranean fleet was withdrawn from Malta to Alexandria out of the range of Italian aircraft, the superficially cynical Hoare-Laval Agreement proposed the partition of Abyssinia, almost the last free African state. When this practical solution was rejected by an outraged British public, pressure grew for the application of an oil embargo. This, if applied, might well have been effective. But it might also have involved Great Britain in war with Italy. As the danger from Germany became more apparent, and the hopelessness of Abyssinian resistance was realized, the pressure subsided. War was averted. But in Britain guilt over our former treatment of Italy was exchanged for guilt over our present treatment of the League.

The result of these compromising policies was, ironically, to bring Italy and Germany together. Belligerent champions of revision, they now formed the Rome-Berlin Axis pointing sinisterly at Suez. Hitler snapped his fingers at the bonds of Versailles and the two dictators, confirmed in their technique, now joined hands to reshape the map of Europe and Africa in the interests of their "young and vital" imperialisms. The conclusion of the German-Japanese Anti-Comintern Pact in November 1936 was startling enough. With Italy alienated as well, Britain and France were faced with the fact that their united navies, in spite of their infinitely greater tasks, were barely superior to those of the three "revisionist" powers.

In these circumstances the British Government speeded up its rearmament programme and at the same time sought a *rapprochement* with Italy. Mussolini's appetite had grown, however, and when, in July 1936, General Franco rose against the Republican Government of Spain, he saw an opportunity for both diplomatic and strategic advantage. For more than a century the weakness of Spain had been an element in the structure of British power. Might not a Spain revived, with naval and air power, its guns commanding the bay of Gibraltar and ranging the Straits from Ceuta, dominate the Cape route and close the Mediterranean? Mussolini and Franco took the proposition more seriously, indeed, than Britain did. Italian troops poured into Spain, followed soon by German technicians and machines. When Russian aid arrived for the Government, the Carlist Wars seemed back again. But now Britain was without her Palmerston and her naval pre-eminence.

The war in Spain dragged wearily on until the spring of 1939. By that time Italy had used that country and Britain's anxiety for peace as levers to extort unilateral recognition of her Red Sea empire and her enhanced Mediterranean status. Despairing of a collective security in which she dared not trust, Britain began to fall back on the power policies which had served her in better days. Chamberlain had tried out his policy of "appeasement", the attempt to buy security by concession. Culminating in the sacrifice of Czecho-Slovakia to Germany at Munich in October 1938 and the recognition the next month of Italy's title to Abyssinia in return for Mussolini's conscienceless guarantee of the Mediterranean *status quo*, this policy was conspicuously unreciprocated. Whereas, on the contrary, by intervening in Spain Italy gained a temporary base in the Balearics, across France's African route, Germany a hold over Spanish industry and some strategic advantages in Morocco. Under cover of the Spanish *imbroglio* Hitler completed the *Anschluss* with Austria (March 1938), thereby turning the Czecho-Slovak flank, and launched his economic drive into the grain lands and oilfields of south-eastern Europe. Provoked by the success of his comrade, Mussolini next, when Czecho-Slovakia fell in March 1939, occupied Albania. By this he secured the mouth of the Adriatic and staked his claim to Balkan "living-space".

These were death-blows to appeasement. In the world as it was appeasement was as much a snare as collective security. Only the traditional way remained, and the British Empire girded itself to face its despoilers if there was still time. The nation that had accepted commitments so uneasily even with France or on behalf of the League, now suddenly extended unilateral military guarantees wholesale throughout the crucial east of Europe, to Poland, Rumania, Greece and Turkey, and struggled to entice the Soviet Union to join the cordon against the new Napoleons.

When Hitler contemptuously picked up the gauntlet by invading Poland in September 1939, Britain was strategically stronger than she had a right to expect. She was able to capitalize on the international anarchy. The small powers, it is true, were chaff in the wind; but the interests of the great powers friendly to Germany were by no means identical. Hitler's Non-Agression Agreement with Russia in August had been a numbing blow; but it did ease the Navy's anxiety over Japan. Whatever Turkey did, the worst that was likely to occur in the Balkans was a partition between Germany and Russia which would close the Near East to German penetration. So long as France held firm Italy's increased imperial commitments made her more than ever a prisoner in the Middle Sea.

Much, of course, depended on the ethics of the new diplomacy. Mussolini might well risk far-reaching breaches of neutrality in order to feed German submarines, in the belief that the Allies would not venture to alienate him entirely. Franco's Spain was a broken country; but air or U-boat bases permitted the enemy along its formidable coastline would be a terrible danger. Happily for Britain, Hitler's naval building programme, unlike his air and army programme, had been mistimed. It had not even caught up, except in submarines, with the limits imposed by the 1935 Treaty. Consequently, there was no need for that appalling concentration of power in the North Sea which had disfigured the strategy of the first German War. One conclusion, however, was inescapable. Success or failure would depend on the capacity of France and Britain to stand together.

At first both sides wanted to localize the war. Hitler's successes had all been achieved by dealing with his victims one by one. Britain and France appeared to have everything to gain by improving their naval and economic superiority. The first seven months of "phoney" war was time gained by them in the initially slow process of mobilizing machine and man power; at

the same time they were able to begin the business of the
blockade, intended to be their principal weapon. In the Mediterranean British shipping was temporarily diverted round the
Cape, because of the uncertainty over Italy's intentions. The
effect of the blockade on Germany's war economy can only have
been slight; nevertheless, once it was clear that the Allies would
not make peace, Germany had no choice but to break out of the
encircling naval thongs before the Allies had time to develop
their enormous potential. The resulting fall of Norway, the
Low Countries and France between April and June 1940
changed the aspect of the war. A practically unarmed Britain
suddenly found herself alone and confronted with the kind of
situation faced by her ancestors after the peace of Tilsit. The
chief difference was to her disadvantage. The Navy was comparatively much less strong than in 1807, not so much numeri-
cally but because the advent of the mine, the submarine and the
aeroplane all favoured the land power against the sea power.

Britain was saved from invasion by her fighter pilots and the
fleet that secured their fuel. But this, of course, was not enough
to give safety, much less final victory. Hitler's territorial gains
and his close relations with Italy, Japan, Russia, Vichy France
and Franco Spain made it clear that Britain's own instrument of
economic blockade would speedily be turned against her to the
point of strangulation. In such a situation caution might well
have been suicidal. Nonetheless, it was surely the courage of
supreme genius that decided M_1. Churchill, after Dunkirk, to
denude these islands still further by sending reinforcements
11,000 miles round the Cape to Egypt to safeguard the Middle
East. It was a decisive moment of the war. Had he not done this
then, Britain would have lost the means she had used so often in
the past, of bringing the resources of the world to bear irresistibly
on those of Europe. Nothing less would have sufficed against
Hitler's Germany. Failing this, Britain and her Empire must
have dissolved. America and Asia would have been left to work
out their separate salvations.

When France fell and Italy joined Germany, the strategic
outlook for Britain in the Mediterranean looked hopeless. Not
only were France's coastline, bases and splendid fleet lost to
Britain; there was every reason to suppose they would be gained

by Germany. Spain made it clear that she meant to have Gibraltar back. Italy's large fleet lay in the central Mediterranean; her air force made Malta useless for naval purposes and dominated the Tunisian narrows; an army of 200,000 men in Libya menaced Suez and Alexandria; another even greater force in Abyssinia threatened the southern entrance to the Red Sea. Britain's only assets were her garrisons in Gibraltar, Malta and Egypt and the two small fleets, one at Gibraltar, the other at Alexandria, both inadequately provided with air cover.

The story of how victory was plucked out of this extreme danger must be familiar to everyone. It begins, surprisingly, with a number of successes. While the Italians made their cumbrous preparations to strike at Egypt, Admiral Cunningham's fleet treated its opponents with a bold disdain. Minor successes in July were followed up in November with the attack on Taranto by naval aircraft, which damaged several ships. An action off Sardinia by Admiral Somerville's Gibraltar squadron having a like result, the Italian fleet withdrew to bases farther up the peninsula and left the central Mediterranean to their lighter vessels. In December 1940 General Wavell, supported from the sea, launched the brilliant sustained offensive which in three months brought in upwards of 100,000 prisoners and took his army as far as El Agheila on the other side of Cyrenaica. In approximately the same period Italian East Africa was cleared and the danger to Aden and the Sudan removed. In the spring, unfortunately, this extraordinary campaign came to an end. This was partly because of the arrival in Tripoli of Rommell's Afrika Korps, but chiefly because Wavell was now compelled to divert much of his strength to Greece. Leaving a garrison in the port of Tobruk he fell back on Egypt in March 1941.

The sudden reversal of fortune in the Mediterranean was due to a revolution in German strategy. Like Napoleon before him, Hitler awaited as long as he dared the development of his invasion plans; and when they failed struck eastwards to remove the gathering menace in his rear and, at the same time, to acquire oil. In the autumn of 1940 the partition of Danubian Europe had begun. Russia took Bessarabia. Hitler brought Hungary, Rumania and Bulgaria as "satellite states" under his control. Italian forces thrust out of Albania into Greece, only to be ignominiously ejected by the smaller people with the help of British planes. That spring a German army swept through Jugo-Slavia into Greece. It drove before it the expeditionary force which Wavell had been forced to sacrifice. The Germans had air supremacy. They did not, however, command the sea. A fine naval victory off Cape Matapan on 28 March repulsed an Italian fleet and secured the Eastern Mediterranean. Admiral Cunningham was able to take off 50,000 of the 60,000 men in Greece at the end of April; and when Crete, too, fell to airborne invasion a month later, to take off half its garrison. Operating thus without air cover, the Navy lost heavily; but its "wonderful tenacity in adversity" prevented any further German movement into Egypt or Syria.

Between April and August 1941 German schemes to convert the Moslem countries into satellite states were similarly foiled. Timely British intervention in Iraq, Syria and Iran secured oil wells, pipelines and a useful connection with Russia. On 22 June, however, his Balkan flank safeguarded, Hitler invaded Russia and by the winter penetrated to the outskirts of Leningrad and Moscow and the banks of the Don.

Meanwhile in Africa General Auchinleck, succeeding Wavell, cleared Rommell out of Cyrenaica once again to the lines of El Agheila; but was then himself forced back first to Gazala and finally, in May 1942, to El Alamein, only seventy miles from Alexandria. Here, as at Stalingrad, victory seemed for several months within Germany's grasp, a victory which, dealing shattering blows to Britain and Russia, would have laid open the oilfields of the Caucasus and the Persian Gulf, and linked Germany with Japan. But just as at Stalingrad, the German supply lines were stretched beyond their capacity. A dangerous sea crossing past Malta and the long desert route put Rommell at a disadvantage compared with an opponent whose supply line took the enormous detour round the Cape of Good Hope. In October 1942 the tide turned. General Montgomery scored the brilliant tactical victory of El Alamein and forced Rommell back once more to El Agheila.

For more than two years the island of Malta had been enduring siege conditions and almost unbroken air bombardment. It had to be held. Its central position between Sicily and

Tripoli made it ideal for air reconnaissance and convoy protection, and enabled submarines and bombers to operate from it
against Axis supply lines with telling effect. The Governor,
Sir William Dobbie, organized its at first pitifully weak anti-
aircraft defences and mobilized the entire population in civil
defence. Pounded incessantly Valletta, unlike London, would
not burn. But the dockyards became unusable, fighter protection could not always be maintained from the blitzed airfields,
and the 300,000 inhabitants faced the prospect of famine. With
the greatest resolution vital convoys with food and fuel fought
their way through from Gibraltar and Alexandria in spite of
crippling losses. Enemy agents in Algeçiras or Ceuta saw the
Gibraltar convoys leave. Enemy aircraft from Crete or Cyrenaica
covered the eastern route. During the summer of 1942 the
withdrawal to El Alamein added gravely to Malta's peril.
Field-Marshal Lord Gort succeeded Dobbie. Spitfires were
flown in from aircraft carriers to sustain the defence against the
Luftwaffe. The ordeal was not eased until after Montgomery's
victory. After that, the island resumed its ancient function as a
forward base, but this time for Air Force and Army as well as the
fleet.

At the western end of the Mediterranean Axis plans were
similarly disappointed. The fall of France found Gibraltar
unprepared to withstand a modern assault. Spain occupied
Tangier "as a precaution", and allowed it to become the centre
of German influence in the Straits. Plans were made for a
German offensive through Spain to take the Rock; guns were
trained upon it. But so absorbed were the Germans with invading England and Russia that there was time to strengthen the
fortress and construct a first-class aerodrome on the Isthmus.
The Allies' strongest card was Spain's determination not to
compromise her independence or her North African ambitions
in favour of her friends any more than her enemies. This, and
the tact and the economic inducements of the Allies, was sufficient
to dissuade the Caudillo from going beyond "non-belligerency"
in his support of the Axis.

Relations with France required, if possible, an even more
cautious approach. Unfortunately, Britain's anxiety to prevent
the French fleet coming under enemy control led to the unhappy

episodes of Oran and Dakar, when French ships were attacked at anchor by Admiral Somerville. The consequent embitterment went far to alienate the entire French naval service; but in North Africa generally, considerate treatment ensured continued sympathy for the Allied cause.

A year after Pearl Harbour the United States was at last in a position to mount a major offensive in Europe, and for this French North Africa seemed the obvious starting point. Landings there would enable sea power to be used with most effect and Rommell's army would be caught in a vice. The problem was to achieve surprise and yet not clash with Spanish or French forces. General Eisenhower made Gibraltar his headquarters and took command of the garrison. Unhampered use of the Bay and the Isthmus was essential to the success of the great enterprise. General Franco made no move to deny them to the Allies.

When the landings were made, in November 1942, U-boat sinkings were at their peak. Nevertheless, the great amphibious operation was completely successful by sea and, in spite of stiff opposition from French warships at Casablanca, the Allied forces quickly secured the Atlantic ports and Oran and Algiers inside the Mediterranean. A race followed for possession of Tunis. The Germans won this, however, and consolidated their hold by flying in troops and tanks from Italy. By the end of the year they had formed a powerful second army there. At length, however, Montgomery's Eighth Army forced the Mareth Line against Rommell (March 1943) and the Allies, now supreme in the air, closed in on Tunis and Bizerta in a grim pincers movement. On 13 May the enemy yielded. In all, the Tunisian campaign brought in a quarter of a million prisoners, including the superb Afrika Korps. At last the way was open for the invasion of southern Italy to reopen the Mediterranean to Allied traffic and so ease the burden of global transport which the Allies' war effort demanded.

The invasion of Sicily was a try-out for the projected invasion of France. The Allies spared no effort to make it a success. Bombers and fighters operating from Malta's airfields ensured Allied supremacy in the air. On 10 July American and British forces landed in the south and south-east of Sicily under the shelter of naval guns. While the English pushed up the east coast against the main German resistance, the Americans cleared the rest of the island and closed in on Messina from the west. In spite of the large-scale Italian desertions, the Germans made a determined stand in the north-east triangle on either side of Mount Etna. When the Allies finally broke through in the middle of August, they skilfully evacuated two-thirds of their numbers across the narrow straits under cover of a barrage of gunfire.

By this time Mussolini had been deposed and Marshal Badoglio had formed a government to negotiate peace terms. However, the Germans disarmed their ally's land forces and it was with difficulty that the Italian fleet escaped to Malta to effect its formal surrender on 11 September. The Allies had now to push their assault from the south in the face of German control. Rather than risk landings farther up the peninsula, they preferred the shorter crossings under air cover.

Montgomery's Eighth Army landed at Reggio on 3 September and advanced swiftly up the east coast, occupying Taranto, Bari and Brindisi on the way. An American army, with strong naval support, landed with more difficulty at Salerno and reached Naples on 1 October. On both sides of the peninsula the steep river valleys imposed formidable barriers, and gradually the onset of winter and the difficulty of supply bogged the Allies down. A landing at Anzio, though threatening Rome, failed to turn the enemy position. Rome did not fall until 4 June 1944 after a skilfully fought spring campaign.

If the Mediterranean offensive had thus lost much of its impetus, it had already achieved its main purpose. The collapse of Italy restored to Allied shipping the freedom of the Mediterranean, and the saving thus made, together with the virtual conquest of the U-boat in the Atlantic, enabled the Allies to prepare optimistically for the Normandy landings. Eisenhower and Montgomery and several divisions of their troops were withdrawn from the Italian front, and, after the fall of Rome it became a question whether the Italian campaign should be persevered with in view of the greater promise in France.

The Italian front was assigned a secondary role. It constituted a useful containing movement and gave opportunity for heavy strategic bombing of Bavaria and Rumania. In August 1944 French and American forces landed in the south of France under cover of a heavy naval bombardment. They met little resistance. The assault from the south coincided with the Allied break-through in Normandy and opened the great port of Marseilles for the use of Eisenhower's voracious commissariat. In October a small British force landed at Patras to hasten the liberation of Greece, the Russian advance having enforced a general German withdrawal from south-east Europe and cut off Rumanian oil. In Italy, the Germans stuck determinedly to the Gothic Line about Bologna for ten months, until the tremendous offensives in France and Russia brought the Allies across the Rhine and Oder. In April, the army of Italy stormed the Gothic Line, crossed the Po, and raced for the Brenner, Trieste and Genoa. Mussolini was murdered by partisans and on 2 May General Alexander received the surrender of the remaining German and Italian forces.

CHAPTER IX

THE IONIAN ISLANDS, MALTA AND GIBRALTAR, 1815-1950

The Ionian Islands

BY the Treaty of 5 November 1815 Britain agreed to hold the Ionian Islands on somewhat ambiguous terms which suggest the modern Mandate. The freedom of an independent state (Art. 1) might conceivably have been reconciled with Britain's "protection" (Art. 2) but scarcely with her "approbation" and "particular solicitude" for its constitution, laws and administration (Art. 3). As a safeguard for Ionian rights, moreover (so it was put in Arts. 5 and 6), Britain was to garrison the fortresses and command the Ionian Army, sharing the cost by subsequent agreement. As at the same time her Lord High Commissioner was to summon and direct the work of the Constituent Assembly it can be seen that every inducement was offered her to order things to suit herself. It can also be seen that the protector was left very vulnerable to charges of violating Article 1.

To shape a course through such an uncharted sea, "King Tom" Maitland was ideally equipped. Strong in Earl Bathurst's confidence, he took over from General Campbell early in 1816 and set about reconciling the spirit of the mandate with his own ideas of benevolent autocracy. A possible rival being the Corfu Senate, he reduced it to a pliable rump by dismissing four recalcitrant members and appointing as its President the firm Anglophil Baron Theotoky. Next, using a Septinsular precedent, he appointed a Primary Council of sworn supporters who were to co-opt twenty-nine others by a double list submitted to the vote of the narrow electorate of 1803. From this Constituent-cum-Legislative Assembly a Senate of five was next elected, with Theotoky added as its nominated President, to serve as combined Upper Chamber and Executive Council. In case some ray of independent spirit might nonetheless intrude, the Lord

High Commissioner retained a right of double veto on all such elections, which, merely by its presence, discountenanced opposition.

No less authoritarian was the arrangement in each island where the native Regent, appointed by the Senate and assisted by a double-list Council, was himself subordinate to a British Resident. The Resident was appointed by the High Commissioner and had, within his sphere, the same controlling powers.

Such was the closely woven despotism which Maitland designed, building on the past, paying tribute to representative institutions, yet capable in the right hands of abating the worst Ionian evils. Maitland genuinely believed, moreover, that such a system would not only give good government but even afford an apprenticeship in self-government.

Although the germs of breakdown were endemic throughout his eight years rule Maitland went far towards justifying both himself and the Protectorate. The islands depending economically on the production and export of currants and olive oil, it was essential for the peasant cultivators to feel secure, which they could never be while the courts were dominated by the landlord moneylenders. Maitland accordingly reorganized the judicial administration on despotic lines. To make the judges more "independent" he paid them better, made them responsible to himself and did not hesitate to break arbitrarily through judicial processes to sustain "right law".

It was equally essential that the Ionian economy should be efficient. Maitland did everything he could to make it so, modifying the law of entail, advancing loans, building roads and simplifying tariffs. This work was assisted by the Greek War of Independence which, by destroying mainland harvests, brought the oil and currant trades a prosperity that was reflected everywhere. Nevertheless, he did not find it possible to relieve the cultivator of his high burden of export duties.

The landlord victims of this policy Maitland sought to attach by other means. The franchise, for what it was worth, remained their monopoly. So, also, the organs of government. There being no outlet for Ionian nobles in the British service he deliberately created for them an elaborate civil service absorbing more than half the revenue, and soothed their pride with

L

Ruritanian titles. So successful was he in these ways, that this alliance with the propertied interest became the mainstay of the Protectorate.

Where Maitland chiefly failed was in the sphere of the spirit. He did little for education, a commodity which Ionians prized, for which Frederick North (now Lord Guilford) was devoting his life and fortune and which might have seemed the pre-requisite of any enlightened administration. Nor did he, in practice, implement the Mandate. The final test of trusteeship is that it should "aim at its own elimination by becoming unnecessary". Both on military and political grounds Maitland refused to advance an inch towards the qualifying goal. Consequently, however admirable his achievement on the material side, it was an affront to the aspirations of all classes of Ionians. The cession of Parga, the strict neutrality in the Greek struggle, made the "free Greeks" of Ionia feel their bondage, moreover, as economic and judicial oppression had never done. To his successors, actually confronted with a "free" Greek state on the mainland, Maitland bequeathed a task of fulfilment beyond ordinary powers.

Down to 1849 the Ionians continued to be governed according to Maitland's dispensation. Their formal history appears as the record of successive High Commissioners trying to justify by good works the contradictions implicit in the Mandate. Roads, bridges, and canals were constructed, shipping, commerce and agriculture encouraged, education promoted, judiciary purged. The islands presented a striking contrast to the Hellenic Motherland, independent it is true, but impoverished, misgoverned and disorderly. It was in marked contrast, equally, to the conditions that had prevailed in the islands themselves before the British came.

Meanwhile, an entire generation of Ionian citizens had grown up, from whom, as Lord John Russell declared in 1840, it would be painful for Britain to withhold full participation in her own freedom. The existing despotism was the more trying in that it obliged the Ionians to contribute a quarter of their revenue to maintain military services into which they themselves were refused entry, and twice that amount to provide a civil establishment from which Englishmen and their satellites reaped the largest rewards. Sir Howard Douglas, Commissioner from 1835-41, protested that their condition savoured of a "conquered and subjected" rather than a "protected" people.

Maitland's successors had not been able to maintain his system intact. Sir Frederick Adam (1824-32) favoured the nobility, quarrelled with the ablest of his Residents, Charles Napier of Cephalonia, and permitted the growth of island separatism by indulging the Regents. Where Maitland had been paringly economical Adam was extravagant. Liberals like Lord Nugent (1832-5) and Stewart Mackenzie (1841-3) were still worse offenders because, by their obvious distaste for the forms of government they were called upon to administer, they excited hopes hardly capable of realization within the terms of the Mandate. The Conservative Douglas, on the other hand, by setting too high a standard for the protecting power, strained the finances, outraged the Church, and estranged the growing class of Liberals. Intellectuals like the historian Mustoxidi and the influential Capodistrias family, disappointed of constitutional reform at home, looked ever more longingly to incorporation in the new Greek State where, if life and property were insecure, at least a Press existed and careers were open to talent.

It was another Conservative administrator, Lord Seaton (1843-9) who took the step which really decided the fate of the Protectorate. As Sir John Colborne, Seaton had quieted disaffection in Canada during the 'thirties and he seemed ideally suited to compose the Ionian dilemma. Believing in the people, admiring the peasant, he soon convinced himself that the Maitland constitution had outlived its usefulness. Its "deceptive" character particularly offended him. He was also influenced by the arguments of Mustoxidi and impressed by the Revolution which took place in Greece in 1843 with British approbation. In his first five years, by a policy of firmness and social improvement, he merely prepared the ground for the changes he had in mind, the only innovations being the establishment of district courts to cheapen justice for the cultivator and a slight relaxation in the Press law.

Then, early in 1848, amid the crashing of European thrones, the Tory despot suddenly launched forth as Radical reformer. Even Earl Grey, most progressive of Colonial Secretaries,

appeared cautious by contrast, with his warnings about steps
that might not easily be retraced. Seaton did not believe in
conceding by instalments. By timely and adequate concession he
hoped to reconcile the "loyal and well-educated" who were
being estranged, and oppose their enlightened and responsible
opinion to the fanaticism of the Unionists and vested interest of
the landed families. If, as his critics lamented, he was driving the
Ionians into the arms of Greece, this did not discourage him.
For many years, he thought, prosperity under British protection
would outweigh attachments of nationality and race. If a prosperous and constitutional Greek kingdom did arise, Englishmen
should surely rejoice to see the islands joined to it. In any case
the first essential was to give the Ionians themselves a free and
efficient administration which would justify the Protectorate by
making them a worthy nucleus of Hellenic aspirations.

Seaton began by granting freedom of the Press, transferring
to the Assembly a joint control of finance, and allowing free
municipal elections. As if to give him pause Cephalonia broke
out that September in armed peasant revolt. But Seaton, convinced the discontent was at bottom economic, pressed on with
his reforms, using the packed conservative Senate as his
instrument for broadening the franchise, abolishing Maitland's
safeguards of Primary Council and double list, admitting vote
by ballot, and allowing trial by jury for political offences.

None of these concessions, it is true, impaired the negative
powers of the Lord High Commissioner. Indeed, Seaton took
care to tighten his control over the Senate, and retained the veto
and civil list. After this, however, Parliament would represent
the Ionian people instead of the Protecting Power and be
directly responsible for the welfare of the islands. It was an
interesting experiment which might in other circumstances have
succeeded. But, as Seaton himself appreciated, the Ionians,
satisfied with their government, might still be discontented with
their lot as Greeks. It was this latter sentiment that prevailed.
Instead of using their new powers to relieve the peasants' burden
and maintain and improve the public services, they were carried
away by demagogic influence to devote their energies to agitation
for Union.

Seaton was a little unlucky in his successor, Sir Henry Ward

(1849-55), to whom it fell to give effect to the new Constitution. Alarmed to find the islanders in possession of rights as yet denied to Englishmen at home, Ward put down the Cephalonian peasantry with floggings and executions which were grist to the mill of the Unionists and brought ironic chortles from Central European chancelleries. Three successive parliaments were resolutely hostile. Impressed by the Jacobin example, Zervos and the Cephalonian "Inexorables" admitted the mob to the debates and cowed the moderate majority. Ward lectured and prorogued them, but they applied themselves exclusively to demand for Union and abuse of the Commissioner and the Constitution. The ordinary business of government went unattended. What with the Don Pacifico affair and the Allied occupation of the Piraeus in 1854 in support of the Turk, Nationalist fervour increased, conspiring with the economic decline to unite Church and peasant, Nationalist and Reformer in opposition to the Protectorate.

In the 'fifties, though there was some alleviation of the economic condition of the towns, chiefly because of the development of Adriatic steam navigation, the recovery of the currant crop on the Greek mainland left the countryside still depressed. By this time also opinion in Britain was losing faith in the Protectorate, while the development of Malta was depriving Corfu of any strategic importance it had possessed. Moreover, a series of petty incidents, including the leakage of a plan to keep Corfu as a naval base while ceding the other islands to Greece, outraged even the favoured Corfiotes. It was decided to send out Gladstone as High Commissioner Extraordinary to inquire into the administration under the Charter.

Gladstone was everywhere received with the respect due to his fame as statesman and Homeric scholar, but he was no whit more successful than his predecessors in directing sentiment away from Union. Yet if political and social reform had been the issue his proposals would have solved the Ionian problem. Recommending a big reduction in the civil establishment, the easing of taxation in favour of the cultivator, and a really independent judiciary, he wanted to turn the "mockery of free government" into a reality by adopting a modified cabinet system. But the Special Assembly summoned to hear him refused to listen. Landowners saw themselves overwhelmed by a turbulent democracy. Nationalists saw the chains being forged to bind them indefinitely to the Protecting Power. The Seaton recipe, having once failed, could not be repeated. If the Protectorate were to be retained now, it would only be by force.

The last of the Lords High Commissioner was Sir Henry Storks (1859-64). By the time he arrived the Italian war had begun, and Napoleon's successes, the glories of Garibaldi, the technique of the plebiscite kept Unionist ardour at the highest pitch. When, in October 1860, Lord John Russell justified Italian independence by the principle of self-determination, he was immediately confronted with the Ionians' claims.

But Storks seemed equal to the occasion. His first two parliaments being obstructive, he carried on alone. Twelve years of Unionist obsession had been materially disastrous. Roads and forests had gone untended, public utilities fallen into decay. The strong hand was now everywhere felt. Through his authority in the Senate Storks tightened his control over higher appointments, threw the lesser ones open to competition, and reduced the powers of the municipalities. Many Radicals, like Zervos, now President of the Assembly, began to reconcile themselves to further years of waiting. Storks congratulated himself on the universal quiet, the material recovery, the good crops and high prices.

Then, dramatically, came the overthrow of King Otto of Greece and the solution of Ionia's problem as an episode in the Eastern Question. By the Treaty of 1863 Britain's candidate, King George, was promised the islands as dowry and token of goodwill, provided the inhabitants were agreeable. Their firm desire being signified by a special assembly in October 1863 and terms having been arranged, Storks formally handed over the islands to the Greek Commissioner on 28 May 1864.

Although the conditions attached—particularly the demolition of the Corfu fortifications and the heavy pension responsibilities—were unnecessarily irritating, it has been, perhaps fairly, said of the story of Britain in Ionia that "nothing became it better than the closing page". Yet it is unfair to dismiss Britain's administration as a failure, even though the Mandate was relinquished without being fulfilled. Her constructive achievement there was very great. The Ionians were easily the most prosperous and cultured citizens of the free Greek State. More, probably, than elsewhere in her Mediterranean experience Britain failed to bridge the racial gulf, but then, in Ionia, among the "free Greeks", where religion and race, separately and together, were prized far beyond all other values, the task was, surely, uniquely difficult.

Malta

When the Napoleonic Wars ended Malta was slowly recovering from the plague. Lord Bathurst and Maitland saw to it that the island secured some mercantile concessions but followed the 1812 Commissioners in putting security first. Malta's political claims were accordingly ignored; and although the vernacular was Maltese, Italian remained the language of Church, courts and schools, English of the administration, whose higher posts were removed from Maltese hands. While to appease the nobility Maitland deliberated multiplied nominal employments and founded the Order of St. Michael and St. George.

The island's recent prosperity being linked with the *entrepôt* trade, Maitland put commercial before other interests. Significantly the 1812 Report had said little of the landed interest, whether noble proprietors with their sense of political grievance or the impoverished peasants and labourers who formed the body of the rural population. When the grain monopoly was abolished in 1822 duties were levied on wheat, a tax which fell most heavily on the classes least able to bear it. Soon bringing in a third of the total revenue, this remained essentially unaltered for a hundred years, the keystone of Malta's solvency.

It was perhaps as well that Maitland died suddenly in 1824 before his reforms had time to take root. Their immediate effect had been to reduce corruption and speed up procedure, especially in commercial matters. He left behind him a reputation for order, integrity and good works which was a new thing in that part of the Mediterranean. But he left also, implicit in such a system, an evil psychological legacy. The Maltese insisted with justice that the King of England had become their sovereign at their invitation and upon their terms. They were consequently dismayed to find themselves subject to a form of government which Britain generally reserved for conquered colonies or convict settlements, and so discriminated against socially as to be a degraded class in their own country. Refused, moreover, the normal channels of protest through a free Press or an assembly, their case was growing pathological.

Under Maitland's successors administration became more lax and life very pleasant for the well-to-do. But Malta did not recover its prosperity and could not stand up to the economic distress caused by the Greek War of Independence, which stopped all trade with the Eastern Mediterranean. Various palliatives were tried to meet the crisis, but the underlying fact was clear that an island of 120,000 inhabitants, only a quarter of them settled on the land and directly productive, was hopelessly overcrowded. Somehow an "invisible export" had to be found comparable to the contributions formerly received by the Knights of St. John.

Stimulated by this distress and by infection from Mazzinian republicanism in Italy, came agitation for political freedom. As so often before in Maltese history individuals and groups came together to represent the corporate interest. In 1832, the year of the Reform Bill, George Mitrovich and Camillo Sceberras formed the Maltese General Committee to demand representative institutions; and three years later the Colonial Secretary, Lord Glenelg, tried to meet their claim by setting up a nominated Legislative Council with one British and two Maltese unofficial members. But such a measure satisfied nobody. The "Claims of the Maltese" went deeper than "representation" by a rich landowner and a flourishing merchant. So, influenced still by Mitrovich and Sceberras and by British Radicals, Glenelg agreed in 1836 to send out a commission of inquiry.

The Austin-Lewis Commission got close to the Maltese side of the problem. Insisting on a further spread of the tariff and some lowering of duties, it also succeeded in at once freeing the Press and protecting the Church by a stringent libel law. Like its predecessor of 1812, it reported incredible confusion in the law courts, now due in part, however, to the imperfect execution of Maitland's measures. But as it considered unthinkable the "commonsense" remedy of substituting English law and English judges, it could only advise further codification and reform of procedure. In similar sympathetic vein the Commission went on to recommend the extended use of Italian in education, as the language of culture and the law; and, to cure the psychical ill, the abolition of useless offices and "systematic appointment" of qualified Maltese to the higher posts. The latter proposals were never given effect to, however, as the incoming governor reminded the Colonial Office that the *raison d'etre* of Malta was, after all, to be secure.

The depression gradually lifted, recovery being helped by the tariff reduction and the development of steam navigation with India by the Mediterranean and the Red Sea. Valletta becoming an essential coaling station, the provision of fuelling, repair and tourist facilities brought money and work. In 1848 the first dry dock was opened in Dockyard Creek. An air of hopefulness spread as it appeared that Malta might at last find economic salvation in the services she could render the Imperial trading system.

In the 'forties, nevertheless, political unrest continued as revolutionary activity in Italy filled the island with refugees and conspirators. The Government came under criticism equally for its "despotism" and its failure to protect religion. Riots occurred in Valletta in February 1846 when the sabbatarian governor prohibited the Sunday Carnival. There was friction with the Holy See over the appointment of a bishop; while the creation in 1842 of the Protestant Diocese of Gibraltar with its seat in Malta provoked the issue of mixed marriages, a question particularly complicated in Malta because the canon law was incorporated in the ordinary codes and enforced in the civil courts.

In Malta as in the Ionians the arrival of Earl Grey at the Colonial Office in 1847 marked a forward step in constitutional growth. In Malta he took the initiative. Believing the Maltese "necessarily precluded from representative institutions" by considerations of defence, he nevertheless broke new ground by accepting Britain's obligation to do all she could to honour Malta's original trust in her, and by appointing as governor Sir Richard O'Ferrall, who was both a civilian and a Roman Catholic.

Although the times were inauspicious for constitutional experiment, O'Ferrall was on good terms with the new archbishop and felt justified in persevering with Grey's plans. In June 1849, therefore, a new Constitution was announced, providing for a Legislative Council of eighteen members, eight elected on a moderate property franchise, and ten officials, half of them Maltese. To ensure key services half the current revenue was set aside as a permanent civil list. These arrangements went far to satisfy the ambitions of the dominant educated class, and Malta settled down to a period of active development under a series of enlightened governors.

In 1854 the new criminal code, confirming trial by jury, came into force, and its guiding spirit, Adrian Dingli, was set free to nurse the new constitution and go on to complete his life's work by preparing the civil code. The same year saw the outbreak of the Crimean War with, for Malta, a sudden access of prosperity as Allied shipping, troops and hospitals crowded the island. Dockyard and wharfing facilities had to be rapidly expanded. There was good work for everybody and money flowed freely. It was a moment of extraordinary boom which Maltese still recall.

During the 'sixties, the loss of the Ionian Islands and the development of the Suez Canal project increased Britain's interest in Malta's commercial and strategic possibilities. A series of works were undertaken to modernize the fortifications and extend the facilities for merchant shipping and the repair of the new iron-clad warships. This Imperial expenditure increased local revenue and encouraged governors like Sir John le Marchant (1858-64) and Sir Henry Storks (1864-7) to improve Valletta, tackle the immense sanitary problem, and do what they could to raise educational standards. Although a local Commission of Inquiry set up in 1865 found nothing but blame for the teaching in the schools, it nevertheless advised the continuance of Italian as the basic language of instruction except at the most elementary level. As education alone could alter the balance of social forces inside the island, it was clear that there had arisen within the professional classes to whom the 1849 Constitution had conceded power a vested interest in delaying educational advancement.

With every social improvement, moreover, the pressure of population grew. By 1861 it was already 135,000. The opening of the Suez Canal increased Malta's importance as a coaling station, but, by diverting labour to the wharves and dockyards, this added to the squalor of Valletta and its environs without diminishing the widespread rural poverty. At the same time Italy's commercial progress lured P. and O. liners to Messina, and former channels of emigration dried up as French control extended over North Africa. As early as 1878 the Rowsell Report insisted that a drastic realignment of social policy would have to be accepted unless Malta was to become a vast, diseased rabbit-warren.

In these circumstances the Imperial Government found itself the champion of the underdog and guardian of the island's long-term interests. Britain agreeing to pay half the cost of a big drainage project, the elected members refused to accept responsibility for imposing more taxes or even readjusting the existing burden; and Malta's share had to be forced through by the official majority. As in education so in finance the underlying social conflict was coming to a head.

The elected members continuing to complain of arbitrary rule, Britain agreed to give increasing weight to their views, especially on finance, until in 1880 the issue was joined by the return of the redoubtable Dr. Fortunato Mizzi as member for Gozo. Eloquent champion of "Italianity" and economy, he soon led an anti-Reformist party of six in determined opposition to the official programme. The Reformers' mouthpiece was the no-less dynamic Director of Education, Sigismundo Savona, who wanted fiscal reform and educational expansion with, on the language issue, the substitution of Maltese for Italian in the elementary schools, English for Italian in the higher schools and courts. In 1881 Savona became an official member of the Legislative Council.

To ease this conflict the Gladstonian Liberals in that year set up an Executive Council to advise the Governor and in 1883 the Colonial Secretary, Lord Derby, widened the franchise to include some of the better-off illiterates, the opposition to the fiscal proposals seeming to him proof that those who stood to benefit by them as yet had no vote. Derby also anticipated the later "dyarchy" by allowing no more than eight official members to attend at one time, and instructing the Governor to accept the advice of the elected members unless imperial interests were involved.

Nevertheless, the Mizzi group continued to win elections, and in 1886 the twenty-five-year-old Gerald Strickland joined Mizzi in a direct approach to the Colonial Secretary which produced the 1887 Constitution. In place of the Legislative Council this set up a Council of Government composed of six official and fourteen elected members, of whom four were to represent on the corporate principle, clergy, nobles, graduates and the chamber of commerce. The Executive Council was also reconstructed to include a minority of three representatives of the elected members. This was in no sense responsible government but it did virtually concede the representative principle. Instead of relying on the official members to safeguard imperial interests, moreover, Britain now explicitly reserved for herself the right to intervene by a direct exercise of the prerogative.

In 1889 Mizzi resigned to resume his legal practice, while Strickland was given an official appointment as Chief Secretary. This brought Savona back into politics and it was now he who proceeded to wreck the constitutional machine. Members of his big majorities refused to serve on the Executive Council and it soon became necessary to go outside the Council of Government to fill the three places. Strickland, meanwhile, used his new office to promote "anglicization" as speedily as possibly.

In 1890 some agreement was reached on outstanding religious issues, Sir Lintorn Simmons, the Governor who had launched the new constitution, leading a diplomatic mission to the Vatican. The Pope consented to appoint bishops in Malta only with the approval of the British Government, to improve the education of the clergy, especially in English, and to admit the validity of Protestant marriages in the island notwithstanding the technical violation of the canon law. The question of mixed marriages, however, had to be left unsettled, and for several years the Agreement was violently attacked by Catholics and Protestants alike.

Malta's economic condition continued to grow worse. Algiers and Tunis competed with her as coaling stations, and as ships became larger they found it unnecessary to make more than momentary halts in the Grand Harbour. Population, moreover, fortified by the improved health facilities, pressed upwards until in 1891 it was 165,000 or more than 1,500 to the square mile. Fortunately for Malta, while the *entrepôt* trade fell off, her strategic value increased as Britain began to look again to her naval defences. Work on the great Hamilton Dock, opened in 1892, and growing fleet activity afforded some relief. At length in 1895 Joseph Chamberlain, as Colonial Secretary, perceiving Malta's place in the Imperial system and seeing that Malta could no more do without Britain than Britain without Malta, proceeded to override the interests of the class which representation had brought to the front.

Chamberlain's policy was threefold. In view of Malta's place in the Empire, he believed English language and culture certain to prevail there and resolved to help them forward. He accordingly gave full support to Strickland in his policy of "free choice for parents" between Italian and English as the language of school instruction. Some ninety per cent choosing English, it was only the need to keep Italy's friendship that stopped him from going on to substitute English for Italian in the law courts.

Chamberlain proposed, secondly, to accompany "anglization" with a policy of good works. As Malta's elected representatives still refused to tax their class to provide health and educational services, he overrode their opposition by Order in Council. When they refused to take their seats, he withdrew the 1887 Constitution and returned to the principles of 1849, with an official majority in the Council of Government and no representation at all on the Executive Council. This was in 1903. In view of the worsening international situation it must have seemed when Mizzi died in 1905 that Malta's political future was dark.

But the blow was softened, thirdly, by the launching of a huge defence programme designed to convert the island into a completely modern naval base. The millions expended by the Imperial Government betwen 1896 and 1906 restored prosperity, multiplied wages and revenue, and enabled the public works programme to be readily financed. Malta's "invisible export" was at last being found in the naval needs of a great Empire being brought to bay.

However, by 1906 the Admiralty works were completed and the boom was succeeded by a slump. Obligations optimistically incurred could not be met. Yet population continued its phenomenal rise till in 1911 it was 212,000—a thirty per cent increase in twenty years. One flaw in "Chamberlainism" was becoming apparent. For a small country a modest self-determinism, if attainable, might be preferable in the long run to absorption in the pitiless dynamic of a great Empire. As a Commission sent out in 1911 reported, Britain by her policy had diverted labour from the real interests of the island to produce an artificial and precarious prosperity, and ought consequently to bear the responsibility for a change of policy which reduced a large section of the population to idleness and starvation.

Happily, Campbell-Bannerman Liberals and Maltese Nationalists proved comparatively sympathetic. Local pride was engaged when a royal duke was appointed High Commissioner in the Mediterranean with headquarters in Valletta. The elected members took their seats in 1907 for the first time since 1903; and in the same year the island's dilemma was fairly and sympathetically put by the Under-Secretary for the Colonies, Mr. Winston Churchill. Expressing Britain's desire to work with them for the welfare of the island, he emphasized the need in a fortress like Malta for mutual restraint. Because in the past they had pressed their legal rights too far, Britain had been forced to curtail their liberties. If he were in their place he would not like such restraints any more than they did. Now it was up to them, by their co-operation, to show Britain that a new situation had arisen. "The door is not closed on the constitutional question," he said.

For a short time this co-operation was forthcoming. Mizzi's successor, Azzopardi, kept clear of the language question and pressed quietly for constitutional revision. In 1909 two elected members were admitted to the Executive Council; but in 1911 the failure of Asquith's ministry to concede an elective majority in the Council of Government led once more to political deadlock.

The outbreak of war in 1914 put an end to open agitation. Except for Azzopardi, the elected members refused co-operation. Fortunato Mizzi's Italian-educated son, Enrico, supported the war but, rejecting compromise on the language question, was imprisoned for sedition. But the mass of the people, led by the Church, joined actively in the war effort and enjoyed the benefits of a boom reminiscent of the Crimean years. Malta became a vast Allied dockyard, training camp and hospital. When the war ended, however, it was found that the Maltese had undergone a spiritual change. High prices, sudden unemployment, the war ideal of self-determination for small peoples, all united to produce a social revolution. While students rioted another Sceberras invoked yet another popular assembly to produce a new constitution.

In patient collaboration over two years Mr. Amery, the Governor, Lord Plumer, and Sceberras's National Assembly shaped a constitution based on the principle of dyarchy. Malta was given two governments acting concurrently. On the one hand, the Maltese Government, following ordinary parliamentary principles, had a Legislative Assembly of thirty-two members elected by proportional representation on a low property franchise, and a Senate of seventeen embodying the traditional corporative idea and including trade union members. Ministers were responsible to this Parliament. The Maltese Imperial Government, on the other hand, operated by prerogative through the Governor, who was advised by a council of officials, controlled specific reserved matters such as foreign affairs, and retained discretionary authority over the general field of public safety and Imperial defence. There was a Reserved List. On the language question a compromise was reached, English and Italian both becoming official, the former with priority in administration, the latter in the courts. Maltese was merely permitted in lower education and speakers of it given "reasonable consideration". It is indicative of the extent of class prejudice among the politically vocal that even this measure of tolerance for the vernacular was opposed by the Assembly, though approved by the Workmen's Union. On 1 November 1921 the first Parliament of Malta was opened by the Prince of Wales, and Filippo Sceberras was knighted.

For six years these arrangements worked satisfactorily under a two-party system with Nationalists in office led by Sir Ugo Mifsud and Enrico Mizzi. They stood for the traditional constitutional movement, were clerical and culturally Italianate but, with the possible exception of the Mizzi wing, loyal to the British connection. In opposition were the Constitutional Party, led by Sir Gerald Strickland and Professor Bartolo and supported by a small Labour group. These were "progressive" mainly in the sense that they drew their support from the Maltese least influenced by the priesthood, and stressed their loyalty to Britain and British culture.

In the short run no government could have done better than the Nationalists. They had to their credit much social legislation, sound health and educational services, big housing schemes, agricultural improvement and industrial expansion. Above all they disposed of 30,000 emigrants and administered the finances prudently, even putting by a reserve fund for emergencies. Nevertheless, there always remained the question whether even they were really getting quickly enough to the root of Malta's problem, economic security for its quarter of a million inhabitants. The Constitutional Party did not think so and, led by Strickland, who had created the 1887 Constitution, it proceeded to wreck the Constitution of 1921.

Strickland took office in 1927 with only a small majority in the Lower House and none in the Upper. His plans included a considerable excess of expenditure over revenue and a raid on the reserve fund. Obstructed by the Senate, he appealed to the Colonial Secretary to secure financial supremacy for the Lower House. As Mr. Amery merely permitted the Maltese Parliament to make the change itself, Strickland's difficulty remained. So he next brought pressure to bear on the elected representatives of the clergy, a step that in Malta was playing with fire.

In an instant every controversial issue was inflamed, and the Imperial Government and the Vatican were themselves contesting hotly. Linked with clericalism were the claims of Italianity which, being pressed by the Nationalists, found favour in Mussolini's Italy. Passion ran high. When, therefore, the Appeal Court invalidated all the legislation of the past two years, the Governor decided to postpone the elections and in June 1930 the

Colonial Secretary, Lord Passfield, suspended the Constitution.

The next year the Askwith Commission, arguing that the Maltese had political aptitude but merely lacked experience, recommended one more attempt at constitutional government. However they did advise the substitution of English for Italian to be taught alongside Maltese in the elementary schools. But the elections of June 1932 returned the Nationalists with a big majority and controversy soon centred on this language issue. Mizzi, as Minister of Education, deliberately flouted the bar on Italian and, in a worsening international situation, the Constitution had again to be suspended in November 1933.

Convinced by now that compromise would not work the Imperial Government this time reverted to full-blooded "Chamberlainism". Over the heads of the Nationalists Maltese was submitted for Italian as the official language alongside English; and after the Sanctions Crisis of the Abyssinian War the 1921 Constitution was revoked altogether and Malta reduced to primitive crown colony status, with Governor and Nominated Council. This was in August 1936. Would the people, the common people reached by the new educational and welfare services, respond?

For two years the Imperial Government did its best to earn popular support, and then, in the era of appeasement wisely restored approximately the conditions of 1887. The Macdonald Constitution of February 1939 provided for a Council of Government of twenty members, eight official, ten elected, and two non-officials nominated by the Governor. In the elections the Constitutionalists won six seats, the Nationalists three, Labour one. Alarm at Italy's intentions no doubt influenced this result, but it was also clear that the electorate was impressed by firm administration, good works and the promise of economic security. The experience of the war drove this lesson home.

Malta's part in the war has already been described. The bombs of Mussolini and the Luftwaffe destroyed more effectively than any step Great Britain could have taken the hold of Italianity on the people. Though Mizzi-ites broadcast from Rome, the fortitude of the masses earned them the admiration of the world. In November 1942 Britain promised Malta compensation for her losses. In July 1943 the Colonial Secretary declared he looked

M

forward to the success after the war of an experiment that had
not been a success before, because of the "hatred and
contempt" now universally felt towards Italian influence and
propaganda.

Thus encouraged, all parties prepared for the future and a
National Congress again assembled to draft a Constitution.
Imperial Commissioners were sent out to advise. In 1945
Sir Wilfrid Woods investigated the financial preconditions of
responsible government. In 1946 Sir Harold MacMichael
threshed out with a committee of the Assembly necessary
modifications in the 1921 Constitution. The upshot was the full
acceptance by Britain of her obligation "not only for the defence
of Malta, but for its welfare as a Colony of the Empire". Malta
had none of the natural resources that enabled other colonies
to pay their way, her one great asset being her value to Britain
and the Empire in war and diplomacy. In a sense, therefore, as
MacMichael explained, the concept of "self-government"
hardly applied to her, for she depended for her existence on
intimate relations with a wider unity. The Imperial Government
recognized this by granting £31,000,000 towards Maltese
reconstruction, contributing to Maltese food subsidies, and
admitting the island to benefits under the Colonial Development
and Welfare Act. The Maltese freely admitted it by their ready
acceptance of the dyarchy. In September 1947 the new Constitution came into force, differing from the 1921 model chiefly in
having no second chamber, adopting universal adult suffrage
and substituting Maltese for Italian as the second official
language.

Evidence of the success of Chamberlainism had already been
afforded in the elections of November 1945 when, for ten seats,
nine Labour members were returned. Further justification came
in the elections under the new Constitution. In spite of every
effort by the older parties combined in the party of Democratic
Action, Dr. Boffa's Labour Party won twenty-four of the forty
seats compared with their four. Significantly, however, it was
the Mizzi wing, with seven seats, that provided the strongest
challenge. While the overthrow of the traditional structure of
Maltese society was symbolized in Dr. Boffa's first budget (May
1948), introducing income tax and non-contributory old-age

pensions, it was clear, however, that the advent of social security measures was throwing into even sharper relief the basic problem of over-population.

For Malta no more than Gibraltar can live of her own. A population of 315,000 increasing at a rate of 8,000 a year, however skilfully it cultivates its 70,000 acres of rocky gardens, however profitably it disposes of its lace, its beer and its onions and mulcts the tourist, however loyally its emigrant sons and daughters in America, Australia or Cyrenaica speed their remittances, cannot possibly by such means alone earn enough to sustain twentieth-century welfare standards. It is as the naval and air base of some great non-Mediterranean power that Malta must find her salvation. It is this that fortifies the Maltese in their attachment to Britain. What if, unhappily, on the prospect of peace, Britain's interest slackens in this warship that cannot be laid up? What if, worse still, Britain is no longer in a position to maintain her Mediterranean power?

It was popular awareness of these facts and prospects that divided Dr. Boffa's Labour ministry, with the demand by Mr. Mintoff's radical wing for the island's direct participation in Marshall Aid, and, in September 1950, restored the Mizzi-ites to respectability and office. The emphasis laid by Sir George Schuster, in his Interim Report of May 1950, on the need for a wise development programme, if necessary at the expense of the social services, has brought Malta $2,300,000 in Marshall Aid or half the cost of the new electric power scheme, as well as £1½ millions from the Colonial Development and Welfare Fund. But the Nationalist Borg Olivier ministry, formed on Mizzi's death in December 1950 with Dr. Boffa as its Minister of Health, has not been and scarcely can be, any more successful than its Labour predecessor in budgeting for social welfare.

Gibraltar

In the nineteenth century Gibraltar's history was as peaceful as in the eighteenth it had been stormy. Free-trade idealists like John Bright were even ready, as Stanhope and Chatham had been, to give back the fortress to Spain as an act of belated justice. For, ironically, the very absoluteness of Britain's naval

M*

and commercial hegemony inclined her statesmen to undervalue
the fortress that had done so much to win that supremacy for
her. During more than half the century Gibraltar was primarily a trading interest and that chiefly in contraband, the
Ferdinand VII whom Wellington had restored setting up higher
tariff barriers than even Spain had known before. Direct trade
fell off and goods were increasingly forced in through Portugal
and Gibraltar; while at the same time the fortress resumed its
role as *entrepôt* between Spanish motherland and colonies now
in revolt. Absorbed in the colonial wars and, after 1820, dis-
traught by revolution at home, Spain became the helpless target
of Gibraltar's armed and experienced smugglers working hand
in glove with political adventurers. Up to two million pounds
worth of British manufactures, mainly textiles, and between six
and eight million pounds weight of tobacco were disposed of in
this way yearly.

It is not easy to say when these great days of smuggling
ended. In the 'sixties the merchants produced unofficial figures
to prove that tobacco smuggling had stopped by 1850 and been
superseded by a more extensive "licit" trade, chiefly in cottons,
with Spain and Morocco. But this was far from being the view of
a governor of the period who deplored the stream of human
beings leaving the fortress "swathed and swelled out with cotton
manufactures and padded with tobacco". Nor had the situation
markedly altered by the end of the century.

If smuggling was thus the chief industry of Gibraltar, it is
not surprising that a gulf was maintained between the civil
population and the garrison. Governors lamented the unhappy
relations which resulted with official Spain and feared for the
safety of the fortress as the "mongrel motley dangerous" population increased. In the early years only a limited British community carried weight, exercised through the Exchange Committee formed in 1817, the smaller foreign and native traders
faring as best they could. The bulk of the inhabitants earned a
living in the boats or on the wharves, or as shopkeepers, huck-
sters and servants. So organized, the merchants were a formidable interest and asserted their right to conduct a "legitimate"
trade, even implying through their agents in the British Parliament that it was Britain's duty to help break down Spain's

"immoral" tariff barriers. But as the century wore on the mercantile community became less exclusively British, alternative interests to smuggling developed, and a more homogeneous community appeared to which, in time, the British Government was bound to make administrative concessions.

When the Napoleonic Wars ended the governor was General Sir George Don, an autocrat like Maitland in Malta, whose first task was to bring the plague to an end. Don is best know for his great achievement in modernizing and beautifying the disreputable shanty town. The fine civil hospital, the public exchange, the police establishment, the sewage and scavenger departments, an improved water supply, the conversion of the burning Red Sands into the cool and delightful Alameda Gardens, the construction of the Anglican Cathedral—all this was Don's work. But to him also belongs much of the credit for the 1830 judicial reforms which set up a Supreme Court with a resident Chief Justice, thereby recognizing that even in a fortress the forms of civil liberty need not be sacrificed to normal military requirements.

The civil population having thus improved its condition and increased in numbers to about 15,000, during the 'forties the fortifications were extended and modernized, port facilities improved, the lighthouse built at Europa Point, and the New Mole lengthened to give securer anchorage. In the same period the advent of steam navigation gave Gibraltar original value as a coaling station. Development was slow but the role essential, the early steamers using their fuel so inefficiently.

The Russian crisis and the Crimean War coincided with the governorship of a general who modelled himself on Humphrey Bland, Gibraltar's legislator of a century before. Sir Robert Gardiner was justifiably anxious for the safety of the garrison in face of an unruly civil population greatly outnumbering it. Thinking it wrong and mistaken to alienate Spain by permitting the illicit trade, he tried between 1849 and 1855 to reassert military supremacy. The merchants, on the contrary, organized in the Exchange Committee and supported by British Radicals and Chambers of Commerce, demanded a consultative council of inhabitants to advise the Governor, and were successful in having Gardiner recalled and instructions issued to publish ordinances in draft so as to give opportunity for local comment on them.

Living conditions remained poor throughout the century. The business part of the town had grown up haphazardly, and the Spanish-type houses with their English-type furnishings and enclosed patios were most unsuited for a congested population in a muggy atmosphere. They let in the heat, but retained the damp, the dirt, and the vermin. The visitor in the 'forties sighed for the "cool penury of Algeçiras". The malignant Mediterranean fever was endemic. In 1866 a civilian Sanitary Commission was set up to improve sanitation and increase the water supply, which in the summer months afforded no more than a quart per person daily. This Commission could do little, however, until in 1891 it was reconstituted to give the Governor and the Services a preponderant voice on it. From that date Gibraltar began to be reckoned healthy, though its housing squalor was still largely untouched.

The transformation of Old Gibraltar into New took place between 1870 and 1900. With the opening of the Suez Canal Gibraltar became the Empire's greatest coaling station and, as such, industrialized. The great defence programme of the 'nineties maintained this prosperity in spite of a decline in the *entrepôt* trade and in smuggling. Between 1893 and 1905 the naval dockyard was completed and the Admiralty harbour of 440 acres enclosed by extending the North and South Moles and adding a detached mole as breakwater and torpedo trap. Gibraltar became pre-eminently a naval station as it had never been before. At the same time the Colonial Hospital was built and the town renovated by the construction of huge water reservoirs, the provision of an excellent sewage system and the installation of electric light.

With the need of labour for coaling and for the Admiralty and municipal works, the population had risen to nearly 20,000 by the turn of the century. The adjacent Spanish village of La Linea became a huge dormitory suburb from which 10,000 workmen came in daily. Strikes among the coal labourers coinciding with the advent of the tourist, a drive was made by the Government to reduce the resident population. Poor and wealthy alike were encouraged to move across the border, but about 15,000 remained.

During the 1914-18 War Gibraltar flourished economically and surpassed all previous records for coaling. But here, as in Malta, the end of the war produced a crisis. Industrialization had been accompanied by the growth of a relatively skilled proletariat, English and native. Work now fell off. Oil was replacing coal, mechanical succeeding manual labour. While prices remained high, wages fell very low. There were strikes, and in 1919 the Gibraltar British Workmen's Association was formed to agitate for better conditions. Already a degree of local solidarity had grown up, fostered by the newspapers in Spanish published in the garrison and by the resentment felt at every social level against English aloofness and military rule. So in 1919 there occurred a united effort to obtain greater local participation in municipal affairs.

Approached by a Workmen's Delegation in London, Mr. Amery agreed to grant them as much self-government as security would allow. So in 1921 a City Council of nine members, five ex-officio and four elected, was set up to succeed the Sanitary Commission in the administration of urban affairs, apart from police, education and hospitals which were left in the Governor's care. By good electioneering the Workmen's Association monopolized the elected seats and so established a right to share with the Exchange Committee the representation of public opinion. The following year a further step was taken when a consultative Executive Council was set up to advise the Governor. Gibraltar had its foot on the Imperial constitutional ladder, if only on the bottom rung.

Between the wars Gibraltar was comparatively prosperous. What was lost in reduced coaling and dockyard activity was made up by developments in the tourist traffic, improved oil fuelling facilities, and the stimulation of small local industries. Imports from Britain still stood at upwards of a million pounds worth annually, but were mostly for local consumption and much less in quantity than before. There was still some re-export trade to Spain and North Africa. The absence of customs duties except on tobacco and strong drink kept the cost of living down and permitted the labouring classes to subsist on their staple vegetarian diet at wages of thirty shillings a week. Health remained good, but housing posed difficult engineering problems. In 1929 the City Council undertook the construction of blocks of flats adapted to the climate and the gradient; but the internal disturbances in Spain, culminating in the Civil War (1936-9) made the problem still more urgent, for as many as 10,000 refugees poured into the garrison. While most of these were repatriated, the English had to be absorbed, and population again rose to 20,000. At the same time class differences between the working Gibraltarians on the one hand, and the officials and wealthy on the other, were more sharply underlined, the one being Republican in sympathy, the other preferring General Franco. Out of this cleavage grew a renewed demand for more representative institutions.

Then came the war with Nazi Germany. Gibraltar became a fortress again, the Governor taking over the City Council's functions and the Executive Council being revoked. While 16,000 non-combatants were evacuated, for those that remained there was good work and high wages. Unhappily, neither in Jamaica nor in England were the evacuees adequately cared for. By a bitter irony the women and children in Kensington received the full weight of London's blitz while the menfolk went unscathed at home. In these circumstances an Association for the Advancement of Civil Rights was founded in 1942. Organized largely by native Gibraltarians it sought to mobilize opinion against the administration on social and political issues. When in December 1944 the Coalition Government put forward limited constitutional proposals, the A.A.C.R. demurred and, with the support of the Exchange Committee and the Trade Union Council, itself approached the Colonial Office. As a result in August 1945 a City Council of thirteen members, seven elected, was set up with wide local powers. In the ensuing elections, based on adult suffrage, the A.A.C.R. won every seat and so, in effect, confronted the administration with an anti-Government bloc.

Since 1945 housing, education and other social services have been pushed forward, but the population has gone up to 25,000 and the cost of living is higher than ever before. There has been much distress and discontent. In 1948 Lord Listowel visited

Gibraltar and, in spite of his fears of "over-government", finally agreed to the A.A.C.R.'s claim for the establishment of a Legislative Council with official and elected members equally represented on it. This was opened by the Duke of Edinburgh on 23 November 1950.

Meanwhile, however, in remorseless tradition, issue was joined between Motherland and Colony over taxation: whether as the Colonial Office believed, there should be a differential tax on profits, or merely, as the Chamber of Commerce and the A.A.C.R. unsuccessfully contended, an undifferentiated license duty on the right to trade. The additional revenue needed to finance the loan portion of the £2½ million housing programme has been found, in practice, by resort to a state lottery, bringing in as much as £80,000 a year. Like Malta, Gibraltar has received benefits under the Colonial Development and Welfare scheme, the chief of which is a project for an 'Atlantic Fishery'.

Within its limits as an Imperial fortress Gibraltar treads the road of self-determination. Somewhere a line will have to be drawn. Beyond that line the ancient fortress will remain Britain's responsibility.

EPILOGUE

IT is somewhat venturesome to attempt to single out the significant strands of development since the close of this second devastating German war. What one sees, however, strongly suggests that the Mediterranean is continuing to exercise its traditional role. The distribution of world power has, of course, altered tremendously, at any rate for the time being. Europe, and with it Britain herself, remains in eclipse. The world has become one world with two great competitors for supremacy in it, contending physically along the entire periphery of the Eurasian land-mass from the Behring Sea to the Baltic, and contending morally everywhere. In a conflict of these dimensions Europe appears even to Europeans much more obviously the peninsula it really is.

But whereas, in the first quarter of the century, Britain deliberately shared her Mediterranean responsibility with France and even, after a manner, with the League of Nations, the course and the effect of World War II have alike entailed the unloading of much of this responsibility upon the U.S.A., itself the spearhead of the latest 'democratic' security system —U.N.O. and its principal arm, N.A.T.O.

Developments since 1945 have included American resuscitation of Western Europe through the Marshall Plan (1947–52), the attempted military organization of Western Europe, including Germany as far as the Elbe, in the North Atlantic Treaty Organization, and the assumption by the United States within the Mediterranean itself of a series of burdens hitherto borne primarily by Britain. Thus the republican U.S.A. has persisted in her strategic friendship with the anti-republican Spain of General Franco. American diplomacy has treated with the utmost tact Anglo-French difficulties with the resurgent Moslem world from Morocco and Tunis at the one end to Egypt and Persia at the other. The United States has stepped into Britain's shoes as the benefactor of Italy, Greece and Turkey and, with bases available in Gibraltar and Malta, seeks to consolidate the Southern Command of N.A.T.O. and to organize a similar Middle Eastern Command so as to close to Russia the gateways of Bosphorus, Suez and Persian Gulf.

It is more than probable that Britain's dominion of the Western Mediterranean has drawn to a close. But the purposes which that dominion has for centuries served show every sign of being secured still by the intervention of yet another non-Mediterranean power, in close alliance with Britain herself.

SUGGESTIONS FOR FURTHER READING

General

FOR the general narrative, see the standard histories. These can be found by reference to the bibliographies attached to the volumes of the *Oxford History of England*, and it would be tedious to enumerate them. Certain works, however, deserve especial mention. *England in the Mediterranean* (1603–1713), 2 vols., 1904, by Sir J. Corbett, and *England under Queen Anne* (1702-14), 3 vols., 1930-4, by G. M. Trevelyan, are comprehensive and definitive. A popular trilogy by Arthur Bryant covers ably the Great War with France. *Statesmen and Sea Power*, 1946, by Sir H. Richmond, gives the naval perspective. *Gibraltar in British Diplomacy in the Eighteenth Century*, 1942, by S. Conn; *Before the War*, 2 vols., and "British Foreign Policy, 1919-39" in *Studies in Diplomacy and Statecraft*, by G. P. Gooch; and *A Short History of International Affairs* (1920-39), 1942, by G. M. Gathorne-Hardy, are indispensable for the diplomatic background. There are excellent short histories of the two German wars by C. R. M. F. Cruttwell and Cyril Falls respectively. P. Masson's vast works on French trade with the Levant and North Africa in the seventeenth and eighteenth centuries are extremely valuable. *British Policy towards Morocco* (1830-65), by F. R. Flournoy is useful. So are *Gibraltar and the Mediterranean*, 1939, by G. T. Garratt and *The Mediterranean in Politics*, 1939, by E. Monroe.

Individual Colonies

R. M. Martin's *History of the British Colonies*, Vol. 5, 1835 edition, gives much contemporary information about Gibraltar, Malta and the Ionians. *Tangier* (1661-84), 1907, by E. M. G. Routh is a first-rate study. Nothing so complete has been done for any other colony. On Gibraltar the best material is in *History of Gibraltar*, 1862, by F. Sayer. *Gibraltar* (1938 edition), by E. R. Kenyon, is also useful. "Gibraltar: Colony and Fortress", by R. Preston, in *Canadian Historical Review*, 1946, pp. 402-23 is indispensable for the more recent period. There is a brief history by H. W. Howes (1946) and much useful information in *Malta and Gibraltar Illustrated*, 1915, edited by A. Macmillan. J. Drinkwater's *History of the Late Siege of Gibraltar*, 1785, is a classic.

On Malta there is W. Hardman's documentary *History of Malta*, 1798-1815, 1909, and A. V. Laferla's sound factual survey *British Malta*, 1800-1921, 2 vols., 1935-47. W. K. Hancock's *Survey of British Commonwealth Affairs*, Vol. 1, 1937, pp. 406-28, has a useful interpretation. Other material may be gleaned from the many government reports.

There is no satisfactory account of Britain in the Ionian Islands. *The Colonial Administrations of Sir T. Maitland*, 1939, by C. W. Dixon, is excellent on its subject. *Four Years in the Ionian Islands*, 1864, by Viscount Kirkwall; *The Ottoman Empire*, 1801-1913, 1913, by W. Miller; *Life of Gladstone*, Vol. 1, 1903, by Lord Morley; and the *Edinburgh Review*, 1853, pp. 41-87, art. by Lord Seaton, are also useful.

The best accounts of Britain in Corsica are *Les Anglais dans La Méditerranée: une Royaume anglo-corse*, 1896, by M. Jollivet; and "British Rule in Corsica" in *Pitt and Napoleon*, 1912, by J. H. Rose.

For Minorca the best published account is still the sketch in *Lost Possessions of England*, 1896, by W. F. Lord. Don A. Victory's *Gobierno de Sir R. Kane en Menorca*, 1712–36, Mahon, 1924, is useful for its subject. *Letters from Minorca*, 1782, by J. Armstrong, gives much contemporary matter down to about 1742.

There are useful special bibliographies in *Documents Relating to the International Status of Gibraltar*, 1934, by W. C. Abbott; "Some Notes on the Balearic Islands", by T. Solberg, in *Papers of the Bibliographical Society of America*, Vol. 22, Part 2, 1928; and in the *Cambridge History of the British Empire*, Vols. 1 and 2.

Some of the more important official reports, etc., are referred to in the text.

INDEX

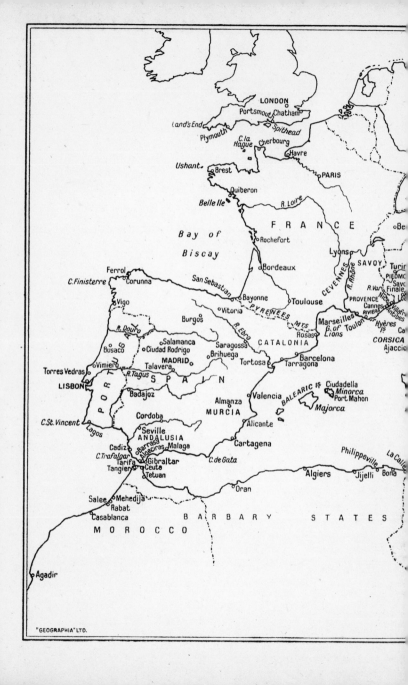